If
This Be Love

Also By The Author

THE SINGER TRILOGY
The Singer
The Song
The Finale

THE VALIANT PAPERS

THE PHILIPPIAN FRAGMENT

ONCE UPON A TREE

THE SINGREALE CHRONICLES
Guardians Of The Singreale
Star Riders Of Ren
War Of The Moonrhymes

If This Be Love

Calvin Miller

1817

HARPER & ROW, PUBLISHERS, SAN FRANCISCO
CAMBRIDGE, HAGERSTOWN, NEW YORK, PHILADELPHIA
LONDON, MEXICO CITY, SÃO PAULO, SYDNEY

Biblical quotations, unless otherwise noted, are from the *King James Version* of the Bible.

IF THIS BE LOVE. Copyright © 1984 Calvin Miller. All rights reserved. Printed in the United States of America. No part of this book may be used or reproduced in any manner whatsoever without written permission except in the case of brief quotations embodied in critical articles and reviews. For information address Harper & Row, Publishers, Inc., 10 East 53rd Street, New York, NY 10022. Published simultaneously in Canada by Fitzhenry & Whiteside, Limited, Toronto.

FIRST EDITION

Designed by Nancy Benedict
Illustrations by Joan Sutherland

Library of Congress Cataloging in Publication Data
Miller, Calvin.
  If this be love.

  1. Marriage—Religious aspects—Christianity. 2. Christian life—Baptist authors. 3. Miller, Calvin. 4. Miller, Barbara.
5. Baptists—Clergy—United States—Biography. I. Title.
BV835.M55   1984   248.4   83–48433
ISBN 0-06-065755-3

84 85 86 87 88 10 9 8 7 6 5 4 3 2 1

ONTENTS

TO BARBARA

Love is crystal. Yet, fragile as it is, every romance makes braggart promises in breathy ceremonies. Having never seen the future, love struts in candlelight and whispers in confidence: "Till death do us part." Yet the best love, I think, always makes its promises without stopping to regard the strength of its ardor. Like all the rest, we once made promises, surer at the threshold of marriage than we could ever be within that unexplored togetherness we walked from anniversary to anniversary.

Now we know. Love is not a happening, but a discipline. There have been times in the decades past that I wondered—even doubted—that I loved you. But doubt is not a sin in loving. Arrogance is the grand transgression, for arrogance presumes, and presumption loses all.

Love is a pilgrimage, and pilgrimages have many endings. Therefore, a book like this risks everything! Either of us could turn in time and shrug away promises once made. In such an hour we might disclaim what we now endorse in joy.

Now, indeed, we honor all the promises we've

made. And since we well know the penalties of neglect, we trust ourselves to discipline our lives and make them work at keeping older promises. It is the older promises that are the hardest to honor. The recent promises are ever nearer and more clamorous. Yet when the fire is low and we are much alone, I hear those twenty-five-year-old words and pledge myself to keep them. My silent grin always means that I am remembering old vows with newer pledges. For in a time where nothing is certain or safe, we both owe our world the kind of risk we take. Here in the hurried days of mid-marriage, I trust the future and myself. Here is the declaration of a pilgrim who has not finished his pilgrimage—though he is hopeful that the end will keep the present glory.

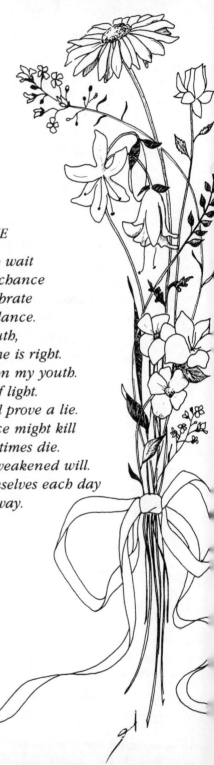

IF THIS BE LOVE

If this be love, expect me not to wait
One day to tell of it. For life is chance
And so unsure that I must celebrate
It while I have the strength to dance.
Here is integrity: If there be truth,
As I can know the time, the time is right.
The passing years have fed upon my youth.
The day to testify grows short of light.
I know the risk: Love could still prove a lie.
Some fickle future circumstance might kill
My best resolve: I do's do sometimes die.
Broken vows are spawned by weakened will.
Old promises must pledge themselves each day
Or, unrenewed, pass quietly away.

1

The First First Lady

She came before you, not in prominence but in time, and yet in every way she readied me for you. To know at first a woman whose very image would be stamped upon your being seems a monstrous strike against uniqueness. Yet here I begin. I knew her first: not just before I knew you, but before I knew anyone. First knowledge emerges unsteady in the haze. It is umbilical . . . inseparate . . . some husky alto lullaby I remember and yet do not. Life dim and far emerges from the womb. It was separate life, yet never separate. An early reverie of gray amnesia, a thereness not yet there. Remembering is not an issue. Being comes from shadows and moves toward the light gradually. Without a sense of self, my knowledge of myself did not emerge as one life but as two. Life was not "mine" but "ours"—the two of us were there at once as far back as I can probe the dim fringe of memory.

She was there some twenty years before you. She was there when my father left—when the bombs shattered the balmy air above faraway Hawaii. With her covey of little ones and no means of support, except her two good hands, her strong intention was to serve. She vowed that her life would give life to her brood of nine.

Fear is a tremulous contagion contracted in dread and spread by those who volunteer to quake. If she was afraid, I never knew it. In her confident presence, I never knew there were reasons to fear, and thus I grew up braver than I might have been.

I never knew I was poor either. From time to time, there are those who do spin straw to gold and those who from the thinnest poverty create a sense of strong abundance.

The house my father left to us was unfinished. However, not knowing what a finished house looked like, I was never aware of the uncompleted state of ours. I could tell it was small—three rooms and no indoor plumbing. We burned wood when the Oklahoma winter was short, and coal when it was not.

My mother was such a pragmatist that none of us ever viewed her as a miracle worker. Wood ranges were supposed to yield hot berry pies and overflow with yeasty loaves of bread. For countless winters I stood before that iron icon and learned that abundance is never what we have but what we suppose we have. I was rich as my mother was rich and I never knew the actual poverty of my days.

At Christmas, she would read by the light of a kerosene lamp—which we called a coal-oil lamp—the Dickens Christmas stories. With never so much as a goose of our own for Christmas dinner, we all felt sorry for the Cratchits. In the midst of a life that others viewed as desperate and hard, my mother's inner wealth was a spirit so abundant that it fostered and made real a luxuriant deception: I was rich.

Still, thrift is the kinsman to wealth. Nothing was to be thrown away. I only later saw all that she taught. Life was an economy! Subtle were her greatest lessons. She gave dignity to thrift. I learned to feel pride in constructing the indispensable from things others threw away. A rummage sale bristled with opportunities to keep the winter warm. Hand-me-downs from my two older brothers were an opportunity to wear things that had already proven themselves worthy. There were a thousand things all about us that, in their simplicity, held a usableness that kept us from any need to frequent those pretentious shops where people with limited ingenuity purchased their goods.

She also taught us that we were only managers of heaven's gifts. The Lord provided everything. Our daily bread had come from Him, my mother said, and like manna, lay on the ground to be taken fresh every morning.

Our house backed up to "the tracks." The great locomotives ran only an alley away from our rough-weathered dwelling. The tracks were the parallel footprints of the mammoth dragons that stalked the land in which I lived. They came day and night—the trains—that left me dreaming by the tracksides. I much romanticized the great locomotives. Enraptured, I waved at the engineers who rode the iron dragons like powerful warlords on armored beasts.

I think she knew how my reveries constructed

dragons from these "puffer-bellies" that drew strings of namby-pamby cars down the silver rails. Some said the tracks went all the way to St. Louis and ended in Los Angeles, but neither of these suppositions intrigued me. Disneyland was decades away, and thus the rails held a mysterious enchantment of their own. The tracks were real; so were the steel dragons. So real that their heavy iron wheels would flatten my pennies to the size of dollars. Those same iron wheels sent earthquakes up and down the line and the grumbling steam would rattle every window in our tiny house.

But the tracks were not dreaming places to her. While I celebrated their intrigue, she celebrated their gravel beds where cross ties, splintered by the spikes, held more than rails. The old wooden cars jolted and banged around during harvest. They would leak, and their spillage was the manna—the daily bread—the windfall to our economy.

She would take a pail and a broom and go to the tracks to sweep the spilled grain, and I would accompany her. The grain we found not only fed our meager flock of chickens, but was a staple in our diet as well.

When the cars were full of wheat, so indeed were the rusty barrels behind our house where we stored the grain we had retrieved from the leaky cars. At harvest time, we worked at gathering the immense piles of trackside grain. I despised the practical drive rooted in her thrift. Yet her mundane view of the tracks held life for her little ones.

I know now there is a time and necessary place that makes trains out of dragons and demythologizes strings of cars until one is able to see a kind of life in them. I took the bread for granted and supposed that it only existed to furnish strength for visions. Out of my mother's practical concerns came the bread for dreaming, and she knew that dreams would all degenerate to poverty if her little ones went hungry.

I was the seventh child, born just after the older children had absorbed the slow-departing pain of the Depression. Her firstborn was barely eight when Black Tuesday occurred, and in the painful management of life, she tirelessly celebrated the warm abundance of even that improvident providence. She knew harvest would come. There would be wheat between the rails.

"We are the gleaners," she said as we crossed the fields on the way home from the "far tracks." There was a second spur a mile or so from our home, and we gleaned the distant rails as well as those at hand. The distant rails were always the most fruitful: since the old cars sat longer on those rails, their spillage was more abundant. Thus we crossed the wider fields carrying sacks or pails to gather all the grain we could.

I hated the practical and tedious. There was too little romance in the strain of lifting chubby burlap sacks. I despised the burden. It pressed all my imagination into drudgery. Steel dragons dwindled to ugly trains and life grew harsh. Reluctantly I learned to trade enchantment for bread.

They say every son marries his mother, and though I cannot prove this rural proverb, it does seem to me now that you and she were remarkably alike. You both loved things that should be, but not too much to deal with things that must be. It has always been my nature to dream the turbulence from whirlpools. You, like her, saw well the troubled waters I denied. How much I've had to trust the both of you to tell me where my visions could not swim through cold reality. Yet your honesty, like hers, was compassionate. Her greatness once protected a child, and your greatness, the visions of a too-reluctant man.

And yet, that fond distinction between the child and the man I learned by walking the fields and crossing "the tracks." I cannot, as St. Paul suggests, "put away these childish things because I have become a man." A thousand times no! For in such childish things is wisdom rooted. I think I learned a love of walking as I crossed those distant fields. I know that in the crossing, my manhood was defined.

PERSPECTIVE

Three decades past I skipped along beside
Her. Soul tired—I carried grain and grumbled.
How tall she looked! How large the fields! Her stride
Was smooth. Attempting to keep pace, I stumbled.
She sat the grain where all the grass seemed dead,
And ran her fingers through my tangled thatch.
"Some day the fields will seem so small," she said.
"When you've grown large, the fields will be no match."
"The fields are very big," I said. "You'll see!"
She grinned and kissed my immaturity.
Our shadows were El Greco-esque as we
Trudged on across the endless earthen sea.
She sleeps beneath those fields where she stood tall.
And I, at last, can see the fields are small.

2

$\mathscr{T}$HE $\mathscr{C}$OMING OF $\mathscr{L}$IGHT

My childhood was set in troubled times. There were wars and rumors of wars.

Two events marked my life in the year 1945.

My earliest recollections of newspapers are stark tabloids of war. My imagination ached from the images of death that every journal and magazine contained. By 1943, all four of my older sisters were newly married to U.S. servicemen. The security of their husbands was an unceasing concern in our family. We spoke of little else at mealtime. I learned the weight of the word *war* as our family dealt with it from day to day.

Mostly it was the newsprint pictures that troubled me. When I looked at those photographs, I could no longer change steam engines into dragons. The tracks had become barren, and all of us seemed no longer pilgrims but refugees from better times.

The papers came and went. I regularly asked my mother about the newsprint pictures. Why war? Why armies? Why bombs? Why do the Japanese hate the Americans and the Americans hate the Germans? Why do the Germans want to kill Jews? Why all these pictures of death? Why death?

I remember that in my sickness of heart, I clung to my mother and waited to know what justification there could be. Then came the bold headlines and the big pictures: D Day, VE Day, and finally VJ Day.

The month was August.

Four-syllable Japanese cities were eradicated by a three-syllable U.S. bomb. Terror and radiation were words I learned quickly, if reluctantly.

"The war is over at least—at last. Your sisters' husbands will all be home—and not a one of them was lost!"

"But the pictures!"

"They will pass," she said. "The pictures will change."

Thinking of the August papers, I asked, "Momma, did the bomb float on a parachute?"

"They say it did."

I watched the maple seeds that summer twist in the dry wind and sail and spin like the propellers of P38s and Flying Tigers. I knew the names of planes for they, too, were in the papers, and I watched the seeds fall and thought of the great canopy of the chute that settled over the children of Japan, until finally the blossom erupted into fire that seared the city and her children to silence. I hated the papers and at last would look at them no more.

Still, I dreamed about the settling of the bomb.

In later years, when our lives had become committed each to the other, I would know the Bible. I would learn from learned men in seminary that God was sovereign over men and nature. But 1945 was a year charged with the spirit of Apocalypse. I went to a small church where I learned the popular adventist truth that Jesus Christ was coming again. The events that preceded His coming would terrify and astound even the Pentecostals, who attended the small, weathered meeting house. The fiery sermons of visiting evangelists held images that, to my own young mind, seemed too much like the fire storms of Dresden or Nagasaki.

One night, I walked down to the armory to watch a softball game. A childhood chum who accompanied me had also listened to the doomsday sermons of the Pentecostal evangelists. He delighted in their fiery sermons and listened much closer than I did. He told me all about the horrible anti-Christ who, he said, would begin World War III.

"We will all be forced to wear the mark of the beast," he assured me. "Right on our foreheads, too!" I was terrified by the idea of the beast and his mark. At nine years of age, my friend seemed delighted by his prophecies. "Those bombs that fell on Nagasaki are but the beginning! Bombs are going to fall everywhere!" he said as he leaned against the wire mesh of the backstop at the softball field. I began to feel sick as he pressed on in his determination to enlighten me about the end of the world.

He asked me if I had ever heard of the Book of Revelation. When I told him that I had not, he informed me that the Book of Revelation told of the Battle of Armageddon: "Human blood will run up to the horses' bridles," he said. The horror of his prophecy, coupled with the pictures I had seen so lately in the papers, was too much for me. It was more than my child's psyche could bear.

I burst into tears and cried all the way home from the ballpark. Nothing of beauty remained to me. I was a man in the making, but manhood was not a worthy goal. When men were grown, they dropped bombs on other men and photographed the devastation so that all men might behold the horror.

"Momma," I said when I arrived home, "will there be blood up the horses' bridles?"

"When? What do you mean?" she asked.

I could not go on with the questions, and I was sure I could not face her answers. The image was there and has not left me for the greater part of four decades.

In time, you and I would meet as survivors of these *visions.* Together we would live through the nuclear omen of the Cuban Missile Crisis. Later, we would fill our own bathtub with water and stock our pantry with meager supplies, supposing the days of our young marriage would give way to universal bloodshed. In our early marriage, we would thus commit ourselves each to the other, daring the evil to come. We, like those around us, gradually grew easier with images of nuclear destruction. We had to live with those images. We could have no happiness unless we let our laughter push the Apocalypse away.

The Armageddon symbol which came to me at a softball game in 1945 left me with the vacuity of a dismal proposition. Mine was a youthful, naive battle with existentialism. Still, I think I knew from that night, I hungered for some alternate path of life.

My chum who had gone with me to the game could not understand my madness. He felt I was overserious about the issue of war. I could not understand his passivity. The magnificent horror he described for me at the softball game did not even interrupt the snowcone he was eating at the time. In him was my horror complete. His spirit would grow up to become what I most feared for mine. Were all men only savages whose greatest dreams for the world would result in holocausts that occurred while we busied ourselves with business as usual? Would the fiery exhibition catch us at softball leagues and snowcones? Later I would read what T. H. White summed up through Merlin's lips: "Man is not *Homo sapiens,* 'man the knowing,' but *Homo ferox,* 'man the savage.'"

I knew what I needed: not to survive, but a reason to survive—indeed, a reason to want to survive. There were too many thorns in the nest, and my discomfort led me to many questions.

There must be another race—another kind of men. Indeed, another world whose newspapers arrive to celebrate each morning the dignity of man. Wherever that world was, it was presided over by a kind God who did not believe in war nor permit it for others.

Where was that world?

Where was that race of men?

My imperfect perceptions were soon to be disintegrated by a discovery as beautiful as the prophecy was ugly. I cannot tell you how important my discovery was for me. In this new world view which had become mine, I found the only sanity that exists. With this discovery, reason and meaning both rose in elemental ways to become mine.

Can one feel all of these things at nine years? Does not maturity read back into the past things that the interim years led me to forget? Of course, to some degree this must be true, and now, as a man, I cannot remember how I felt so long ago—at least all that I felt. But the rudiments of these years are real to me—the pain of seeing the papers and reckoning with war. The intensity of my juvenile despair was also real—accentuated by the times I saw my mother fold one hand in the red-white knuckles of the other, asking God to bring her childrens' husbands home.

Near the end of 1945, I went to a "tent revival," set up in an open field near my home. Dressed in denim overalls that children customarily wore, I sat on a plank supported by concrete blocks. I shuffled my naked feet through the new wood shavings that served as a floor for the tabernacle. The aroma of the newly sawn wood fibers and the fall air that filtered through the tattered canvas of the revival tent brought an exhilaration of spirit.

It was years before I would behold the Gothic cathedrals of Europe. In my provincial view, the great tent was a great church. The hymns were as happy as the brotherhood was exhibitionist. Here I found a reprieve from a world too much burdened by the heaviness of Nagasaki and ballpark prophecy. The sawdust seemed sweet and safe and warm to my bare feet. It was a haven where they sang of heaven.

"When we all get to heaven," they sang. Was this the other world I sought? Was it bomb-proof and real?

Perhaps the hymn was escapist. Perhaps it prevented those who sang from dealing seriously with their troubled world. But its logic offered a kind of healing to my mind. Here was a world for me. Could pearly gates and golden streets be any sweeter than sawdust aisles and amber canvas? They sang of a "haven of rest" and I knew it was true. I had found a Pentecostal stopover that was an oasis in parched Armageddon. What a gallant, warless world! This other land was a safe place, a place for dreaming and living and being men. In joy I heard them sing of it.

When we all get to heaven,
What a day of rejoicing that will be!
When we all see Jesus
We'll sing and shout the victory.

I have a friend who refers to such music as being "Blood-of-the-Lamby." Now, I know that it was not the great music of the church. Then, it held an answer I needed. Soon they sang an altar call. Even that was utopian music to my ears.

Two great ladies, rotund as they were earnest, showed me "the way to Jesus." It was a way I was all-too-eager to walk. There, in the smell of new sawdust, I met Christ who became the pier of my logic.

Inner light arrived. They told me Christ had saved my soul. It was not my soul alone He had saved, but my whole world view. Despair fled. The newspapers could no longer extinguish hope. Holocaust knew an answer: He was there, and He was mine.

CHILD OF ARMAGEDDON

A child of holocaust will cry for space
To hide. Despair and insecurity
Make children run and whimper to embrace
Some thread of hope and worthy sovereignty—
I read of war and and distant enemies:
I, Armageddon's child, whose joyless rhyme
Was sung in nuclear Gethsemanes.
Where doomsday was the looming foe of time.
Christ came to be a midwife in the fray
As I dropped womb-ward towards the Trinity.
My childhood knew the birth of God. The day
He came, the vacuum died. Infinity
Was reckless joy and braggart bright
As I, with titan stride, stepped out of night.

3

CRUEL AFFECTIONS

My sixteenth year came, and I was ignorant of your existence still. You were eleven years old and growing up in a rural Oklahoma town some twenty-five miles distant—so close, yet a hemisphere away!

The red shale roads of Oklahoma were soon to give way to asphalt, and when at last they were bladed free of ruts and black surfaced, our worlds would be connected. Our lives, till then, would remain separate.

My need to know you was circumvented by unpaved roads and by those two whose love I knew ahead of yours. Christ was my indwelling counsel and my mother remained a visible symbol whose nearer image had become a kind of life goal.

Both of them were demanding. Each of them had things for me to do. Throughout my fatherless adolescence, I knew I needed Christ. Throughout childhood and my teen years, it was my mother's rustic idealism which made me believe in myself. She was a kind of protoplasm demonstration of Him, and He was the invisible essence of her spirit. Each of them held dreams for me, and I sought to please them both.

The demands of my sixteenth year became grievous. She began to talk to me about a career which would force me out of the home. I resented her continual nudging me to the edge of the nest. When I peered over the rim of her security, I was frightened. I had always preferred life within myself, for only behind the locked gates of my own soul did I know the terrain. Within this warm cloister, I had retreated from the cold sociology of grammar school and the wilderness of high school. I was all angles and thin lines. In contrast to my own under developed self-image, it seemed that the athletes in our small city had all the esteem and acceptance. They were stars not only at sports, but all of life; they ran past my thin shadow in every corridor of my teen years. I was never good at athletics. I could not say if this was because I never had known a father to cheer such interests. I resented my high school years where only athletes held esteem. Mandatory physical education was a four-year course in violence for me. I was good at the language arts, but Latin scholarship held no esteem in our school. Thus, my own sense of self-esteem developed improperly.

Never was I lonelier than in my sixteenth year. Naturally I clung to her, and she sought to push me within a brief year or two toward career. I had no idea what I could do or what I might be good at. Boys I knew smoked Lucky Strikes and talked about joining the Marines. My own skeletal profile was not generally what one saw in the recruiting posters that pictured the "fighting leathernecks."

I could not conceive of a career, and my own desire to succeed beyond the nest was less than my desire to keep warm within the nest.

Still, she pushed.

Naturally, I turned to Him for consolation. "What wilt Thou?" I prayed. The little church I attended was one in which everyone prayed in a kind of Elizabethan tongue, and so did I. Adolescent Gethsemanes often seem trivial gardens to adults. I sought an answer that would deliver me from her harsh pushing. Seeing my tendency to hide from the future, she kept asking me about my career. To escape from her, I turned to Him. He met me in the sixth chapter of Isaiah:

> *In the year that king Uzziah died I saw also the Lord sitting upon a throne, high and lifted up, and his train filled the temple. Above it stood the seraphims: each one had six wings; with twain he covered his face, and with twain he covered his feet, and with twain he did fly. And one cried unto another, and said, Holy, holy, holy, is the Lord of hosts: the whole earth is full of his glory. (Isaiah 6:1–3)*

Isaiah was but an adolescent himself when he received his calling at the funeral of King Uzziah. Like Isaiah, I drew back from the idea. There was the demand of Him who did "inflame the holy seraphim with fire," as St. Bernard once said.

It was not hard for me to call myself a teenager, but it was hard for me to think of Isaiah that way. Yet,

21

he must have run full face into holiness and felt its high-altar demand.

This scripture was old. Twenty-eight hundred years old! For twenty-eight centuries, God had been making big demands on adolescents.

"What right did He have to go around for twenty-eight hundred years terrifying teenagers?" I wondered.

> *And the posts of the door moved at the voice of him that cried, and the house was filled with smoke. (Isaiah 6:4)*

It is hard for thin teenagers to go against such celestial fireworks and survive. It is hard to talk to God when He's fuming and fussing in fire. How could I know what He wanted? Something, I was sure—but what? And could I manage what He wanted? The will of God is never as hard for me to obey as to locate. The Land of Oz loomed large—I found my nest gone, but unlike Dorothy after the storm, there was no yellow brick road for me to follow.

"God, please—if you can't show me the road, at least give me the direction—I'm afraid I will disappoint her and You both," I called out.

She was demanding that I leave the nest; He, that I be a minister. Neither of them let me live through my final year of high school in peace. Loving them both, I could turn to neither for understanding. She wanted the difficult; He, the impossible.

I graduated from high school at last and hired on to a traveling harvest crew. I ignored her by leaving home and read widely around Isaiah 6 to ignore Him. I drove a huge grain truck from the sandy fields of Oklahoma across the wheat fields of Kansas, Nebraska, and South Dakota.

My thin frame began to pick up a wiry toughness that summer, but my mind was ill at ease. I knew that driving a truck would not be worthy of those gifts she believed I had, but I was too entangled in my insecurity to ferret out any self-confidence.

Further, Christ was not satisfied, and I knew it. He was that inescapable "Hound of Heaven." In the wheat fields of South Dakota, as I bent my naked back scooping the golden harvest, He spoke to me till my own sweat mingled with the tears of His proposition. The work was easy compared to what He asked. He drove at me with His own persistent presence.

Wheat, ripe and abundant, poured like water from the spouts of combines, and I knew I could not leave Him or His demands in Oklahoma. He had met me in Kansas—and shouted out above the motor of my truck in Nebraska. In South Dakota, the harvest only suggested the other harvest he spoke of in the gospels. His fields were also white unto harvest—a harvest over which He was Lord and which I had ignored.

August came.

Why did everything always come to a head in August? It was a full nine years after Nagasaki, but my madness was more furious than ever. I left South Dakota and returned home. She who once taught me to carry grain across the wide fields was waiting.

She reminded me that it was only a couple of weeks till the opening of the university. I told her that I was reckoning with Him. I told her I was frightened, but I acquiesced.

I took a small suitcase and the three hundred dollars I had earned driving a wheat truck that summer. She and I walked to the bus station late in August.

I couldn't speak, and she didn't. He was silent as well. I was so afraid as to be nearly morose. I bought my ticket, kissed her good-bye, and climbed into the diesel bus. I waved at her from the window, and the bus lurched out into the thin Oklahoma traffic.

They had won!

With no real hope of meeting either of their expectations, I was headed toward the university. The wheels ground their heavy rubber into the seeping August asphalt as I rode into a future I doubted would ever please them and, hence, could not possibly please me.

"It's absurd," I said aloud above the diesel churning of the smoky bus. Isaiah 6 loomed large:

Also I heard the voice of the Lord, saying, Whom shall I send, and who will go for us? Then said I, Here am I; send me. (Isaiah 6:8)

A grasshopper splatted on the visor of the huge bus.

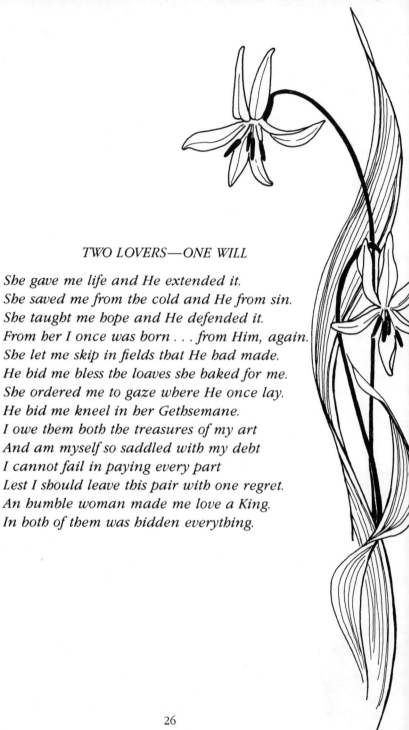

TWO LOVERS—ONE WILL

She gave me life and He extended it.
She saved me from the cold and He from sin.
She taught me hope and He defended it.
From her I once was born . . . from Him, again.
She let me skip in fields that He had made.
He bid me bless the loaves she baked for me.
She ordered me to gaze where He once lay.
He bid me kneel in her Gethsemane.
I owe them both the treasures of my art
And am myself so saddled with my debt
I cannot fail in paying every part
Lest I should leave this pair with one regret.
An humble woman made me love a King.
In both of them was hidden everything.

4

A Muted Monster

You were now thirteen and I eighteen. Our life together was drawing near. My quixotic tilting at giants was never real. But like Quixote, I never discovered what windmills were until all the jousts were over. I had one demon that needed to be exorcised—an ogre that had no voice, for its tongue had been ripped away by fear.

This denizen guarded the way to my profession, determined I should never enter. I could not speak in public. The terror of speaking in public let me view myself only in a comic glass. The fear of some phantom, but possible, embarrassment taught me to despise myself. I became very aloof, always wanting friendship—but afraid of rejection.

I enrolled in Speech 101 precisely because I was afraid to speak in class. I rarely mustered the courage to ask a question. My queries seemed too naive to voice.

I set out on each new assignment in public speaking with a firm resolve to conquer my fears, but my resolutions always ended in failure. If the seraphim of Isaiah had purged my lips, they had not enabled them. My greatest defeats came in the fear of what I knew His calling was.

> Go and tell this people,
> Hear ye, indeed, but understand not.
> And see ye indeed but perceive not. (Isaiah 6:9)

"Telling" may have been a strength for Isaiah, but it was not an attribute of mine. *Preaching* was a demon word, and I decided that the ego force required in preaching might be minimized in teaching. Teaching as a career profession was, therefore, much more attractive to me. Either one, however, still required public speaking. For eighteen weeks, I lived in terror of my speech class.

I had always been taught that self-consciousness was a form of egoism. I knew even then that I lived too much inside myself, but I was so tied by feelings of doubt and inferiority that I could not find any liberation from my own weak self-image. I was not able to cope. I always began with bravado and found myself stammering and giving way to failure and embarrassment. It was a pain not only for myself but for the class as well.

Because of Christ and my mother, I felt compelled to continue the ordeal, even though the agony of the dilemma plunged me into deep depression. My speeches were always manuscripted and they read well. But my delivery of them fell short.

Mercifully, the end of the semester came and the course with it. My professor promised to pass me if I promised never to enroll in any of her advanced courses. Foolishly I promised, only to break the promise because of the inner spiritual pressure. I shall long remember her crest-fallen look when I walked back into Speech 102, determined to do better than I had done in Speech 101.

Again the humiliation, again the awful pressure to resign the course and yet never to resign.

My madness distilled in loneliness. I prayed for courage—the prayer went unanswered. Fear, like cancer, is best cured in the early stages. My struggle was all the more intense because I had waited so long to deal with it. All through high school I had retreated and withdrawn from any position of visible responsibility.

I had to learn to speak, but when I considered that I might be facing the horror throughout a lifetime of ministry, despair settled all the more about me.

Several times during the second semester I vowed to quit. At every plateau of despondency, Christ came—I knew He loved me, yet I fled. I did not want His presence, for it reminded me of my unfulfilled desire to please Him. Like Francis Thompson, I sought to elude the elusive "Hound of Heaven":

> *I fled Him down the nights*
> *and down the days.*
> *I fled Him down the arches*
> *of the years.*
> *I fled Him down the labyrinthine*
> *ways of my own mind*
> *And in the midst of tears*
> *I hid from Him.*
> *And under running laughter.*

I wish I could report some dramatic experience or breakthrough. I cannot.

If there was one single tactic that delivered me, it had to do with the image in my mirror. My professor, whose patience had grown threadbare and whose nerve endings were as raw as my own, told me never to come to class with a speech that I had not practiced out loud at least ten times before a mirror. Videotape was still hiding in the future, so the playback system I used was a looking glass. But there I discovered a third and powerful force that was a determinant of destiny—and I could not turn away from it.

There was in my mirror an angular face—molded like hers—and energized with His purpose—yet different from both. The chin was not weak nor was the eye. There was a strong lip and sufficient volume of air that lifted hefty syllables without breathing hard. I practiced the speech, and my face agreed in strength with the strong content.

That's what was wrong! I had seen her face, so often disappointed as it floated ghostlike before my mind's eye. I had seen His face, lit by the unsteady flickering of my inconstant trust and fear of failure. But I had not seen my own face.

It was odd that I had not, for I had beheld it for two decades.

At last I was able to speak my speech to the glass "trippingly on the tongue." I tried, as Hamlet advised his players, not to "saw the air" with gestures that did not suit the actions. Soon the face eroded and left only my blue-green eyes enrapt with their own reflection. The hypnosis of my own rising ego at long last forgot other issues.

Before my mirror, four eyes gathered into two pairs and my reflected self stared hard and powerfully at my real self. In some ways, I was born before that glass. I came into being by seeing my own self, struggling to be free from any need of approval by others. Once free of the need of it, I received it in fullness.

I have had so many sincere Christians tell me that the ego of a Christian should be annihilated, so only Christ can live in its place. What an unhealthy pietism that is! A theology for worms, not men. Ego is *our* primal being, and when it is crushed, human life despairs its noble kingdom and makes men less than men. Suddenly neither Christ nor my mother were present—only I was there. Alone. I stared strength into the weak image I had taken to the glass.

At once I knew the truth of what St. Bernard had said. It was true that until we love ourselves, we can never be free enough to love God or man. Christ was not angered that I learned to act alone. It was His demand. My usefulness to Him would be determined by my ability to stand and, in His name, to face the beast, whether I felt His presence or not.

I stood at last to speak as one made new. My eyes searched for an object, no longer content with seeing faces. Now they needed eyes. Eyes were the light of faces—eyes were the substance of thought, the mirrors to the mind, the gauges of interest, the shuttered apertures of soul.

I saw, and I was free. My eyes grabbed the pro-

31

fessor's, and I threw a paragraph of content into those unbelieving apertures which grew wider when my words did not dissolve in stammering. I released my hypnotic beginning with my professor only to grab other eyes. Others, too, opened their eyes to sip the vision of my own. In fury, my own face stalked its image in the faces of those who filled the classroom. I was real. I knew the truth at last! I didn't have to pass speech, but I had to *become*. Surely He knew. And He did not want me to anguish in a nothingness that would honor neither of us. Alone I had won.

I sat down. My ordeal was over!

The hydra slain! In this discovery of myself, I was free to love. Naturally, I met you, on the sturdy threshold of myself.

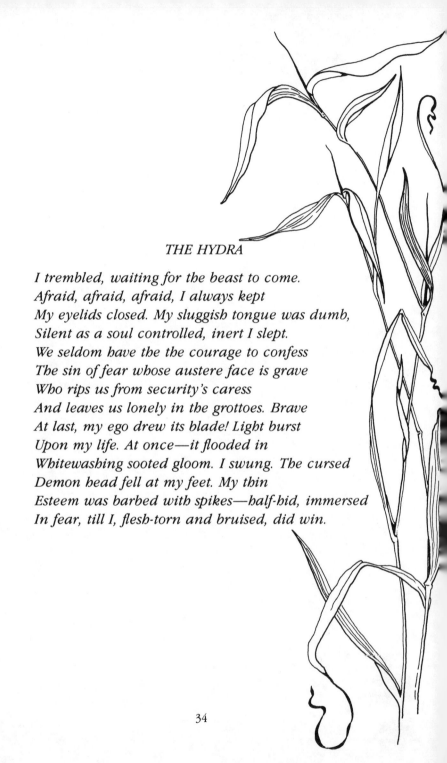

THE HYDRA

I trembled, waiting for the beast to come.
Afraid, afraid, afraid, I always kept
My eyelids closed. My sluggish tongue was dumb,
Silent as a soul controlled, inert I slept.
We seldom have the the courage to confess
The sin of fear whose austere face is grave
Who rips us from security's caress
And leaves us lonely in the grottoes. Brave
At last, my ego drew its blade! Light burst
Upon my life. At once—it flooded in
Whitewashing sooted gloom. I swung. The cursed
Demon head fell at my feet. My thin
Esteem was barbed with spikes—half-hid, immersed
In fear, till I, flesh-torn and bruised, did win.

5

$\mathscr{T}$HE $\mathscr{N}$EW $\mathscr{Y}$EAR

By my twentieth year, Korea had grown stable at the thirty-eighth parallel, and the Russians were into space. These "little" issues were less important to me than my newfound confidence in myself. A year had passed since I had earned my first pleasing marks in speech and communication. The office at the Student Alliance of Ministry had found some opportunities for me to preach. Most of my early preaching was done in rural pulpits where there was no full-time minister. I wanted these pulpit experiences. Indeed, I knew I needed them. With each preaching assignment, my insecurity lessened. Preaching was not easy for me, since I still continued to memorize each sermon before a mirror. Hours of tedious preparation, therefore, were involved in getting myself ready for every sermon. It was on one of these pulpit assignments that my life leaped into the future.

I met you.

It was not love at first sight. I cannot say that I even considered love at all when first we met, but the embryo of relationship was created.

1956 was the last summer I ever drove a wheat truck. No sooner had I returned from the grain fields of South Dakota than I received a letter informing me that a rural parish in Garfield County, Oklahoma, had lost its pastor and needed someone to preach there for the rest of the summer. My arsenal of sermons now stood at six or so, with most of them so thoroughly memorized I could have delivered them in total darkness.

August in an Oklahoma pulpit was a challenge. The heat always forced the windows open, and poor screening invited insects into every rural church. I arrived early that morning before the heat of midday turned the sanctuary of the little church into an inferno. I had borrowed a 1946 Chevy Sedan for the trip, having no car of my own. It was covered with red dust by the time I arrived in a too-heavy suit to deliver my rote, twelve-minute sermon.

I had a sense of exhilaration the moment I walked into the fifty-year-old frame structure. The belfry had years before grown timber weary, and the heavy bell had long been removed. Apart from the renovated steeple, the carpentry structure was as charming as it had been the day it was dedicated in 1903, an incredible four years before statehood. The circular oak pews were dark and rich and held an American Gothic congregation of young and old. Some fifty souls came to church to worship that morning and to hear the first of my six twelve-minute, looking-glass sermons.

Their previous pastor could preach twelve minutes before breathing, and his marathon one-hour messages made my short sermons seem anemic. His appeal, however, had not been as intense as his zeal. When my short sermon was finished, I was already a prime candidate for the pulpit. All six sermons which I owned could be preached, with memorized punctuation, in less than an hour and a half. The board of trustees offered me an annual salary of $1,500 a year to "stay on," and I agreed to stay.

I bought a 1951 Chevrolet Coupe—clerical black—and a suit to match and commuted on weekends to the rural church to be a minister. In my naiveté, I overrated my own importance to the rural community. But without question, the church for me became a priority. I loved the congregation passionately. My ardor was fixed in the joy of the older saints who were sick and infirm and shut off from others who would love and care for them. I discovered an immense number of lonely people—some the sons of the first settlers who had entered Oklahoma when it was Indian territory. The good land and the strong people who sowed it to grain were suddenly mine. My land! My people! I wanted to be in their land and in their lives to do whatever I could for any who had need.

I was so in love with them, that it took me a while to see you. It seemed to me that I was perfectly cut out to be a priest and not a parson. I could not imagine myself ever being able to prefer one woman above the whole of all the men and women who comprised my red-shale bishopric.

Their faces long obscured your own: faces cut by hard winters and sun-blistered harvests, eyes wrinkled from decades of squinting over red landscapes. The men wore overalls, and the robust women could drive John Deeres, milk cows, and manage to diaper their infants with all the tenderness of the rough-chiseled madonnas the land had ordained them to be.

You were among them, but never knew the music I found in hearing them sing their country hymns. Could you sense that I exulted to sit in a pulpit chair and see their faces, earnestly set in rural praise, with hymns that their parents had taught them in buckboards and farm wagons a generation before? The power of their celebration of God moved me, for it was their celebration of themselves—a *gloria in excelsis* to the land and the life that raised churches and windmills in the plains. God knew I loved them!

I worked hard at my sermons, for it was a simple way to delight them, and their delight in any subject was my delight. I was never good at thundering against sin. Theologically, I knew they were sinners, but individually they were of the good earth which came without moral qualification. If the land was good, so were the people.

I learned your name three years before your significance to me began to dawn on my awareness. It's fair to say that you loved first, and with such fervor that I could not deny you loved or honored this most powerful delusion within yourself. I saw you laughing in the vestibule of the church one day, and your laughter was so free that I knew you belonged to these who loved the sky and earth that fed them and supported their frame houses and weathered barns.

I saw you dressed in simple clothes that set you free to be a part of them. We went to dinner in the county seat. I remember how good I felt as we drove the red roads leaving a cloud of dust behind us as we went.

It was right to be together, for we loved the same province and were the grandchildren of those who came into the county in the 1880s and 1890s. My forebears were born in Nebraska when the wagons were delayed coming into Oklahoma. Your grandmother had come to Oklahoma before the opening of the Cherokee strip homesteads and had been there when the county settled itself and the roads were cut. My grandfather had helped open the first railroads through the state.

Of course our heritage was pioneer, and we loved the world we knew. My romance with you was born in an intrigue—our mutual heritage and the people. But your love settled directly upon me. It seemed a narrow focus when there were vast and panoramic reasons to love.

It was here that I confess my ardor flagged. Younger five years than I was, you raced ahead of me to call me your beloved. I declined so narrow and so intimate a definition.

You told me that you loved me on our first date. I never liked the word *date*—it seemed a shallow word to define those portentous rendezvouses that led to marriage. Date—that four-letter word that spoke of contrivances: arranged meetings so that love could get underway.

I did not consider your declaration of love to be spurious or immature. But what was "love" the way you used the word? Indeed, the way others used the word? "To love" or be "in love" seemed an untried, shallow category. Certain movie stars fell "in love" and "out of love" again. One by one, my college acquaintances had fallen in love. In the ardor of their passion, they spoke of the delirium of honeymoons and the ecstacy of their status.

I wasn't sure what "love" was, but I knew it would not work if only one of us claimed it. Still, it seemed sufficiently strong with you; I could not doubt its domination of your world view. You taught me there was that special substance in *eros.* You made me believe that it existed. I felt guilty for not having found it in myself when it was so obvious in you. I could easily see the stars in your young eyes. But your eyes caught some glistening light that mine missed.

Nonetheless, a marvelous security caught hold of me. I had been loved twice by two women who spanned three generations, for my own mother was, indeed, beyond mid-life when I was born and yours was barely old enough to be a mother when you took independent life.

Twice loved by women who were remarkably alike and who for some odd reason had such affection for me as to *exalt* my mediocrity and see such potential in my weakness that it often embarrassed me.

A strange feeling of glory occupied me. The custody of the older woman's affection released me eagerly to the younger. The older woman would not quit loving me, but she felt an excellence as though she was surrendering a life prize to the romantic, untried love of the novice you were.

My own mother, made strong by life in the plains, insisted that *love* was a word with no right to itself until it had been tried in the crisis of laboratory hardship. She defined her love in systematic sacrifice, and as she surveyed you, she knew you held solid, if untried, affirmations of the same definition.

I wished that I desired and craved the same knowledge of the love you felt and assured me was there. Such "falling in love" eluded me, and I could only stumble into liking. But your obvious affection won my confidence. There was born in me the strong desire to keep the treasure that you called love and offered gladly unto me.

I loved your being in love with me and gambled with a trust that one day this elusive substance, which was so definite for you, would be definite for me as well. It was on a January day in 1959 that I bought the ring and I picked the cedar-lined lane by your old homestead as the perfect place to give it to you. It was the perfect occasion. You loved me and I felt good about it.

OF CERTAINTY AND DOUBT

You came to me, for I was less convinced
Than you that you and I were meant to be.
How could you know that confidence you sensed
Would justify your sense of prophecy?
I felt the impact of each quality
You owned . . . your ancestry . . . your vibrant love
Of laughter and your firm, unbending plea
That marriages like ours were made above.
What was the chemistry I must have missed?
How could I doubt what you found so secure?
I wanted your assurance when we kissed
That all our fiery pledges would endure.
My unbelieving love I knew must grow.
I kissed and doubted—starved to love and know.

6

$\mathscr{T}$HE $\mathscr{W}$ITNESS OF THE $\mathscr{C}$EDARS

You wore a diamond. The community approved of our engagement, and we saw the approval in various ways. The constable who made safe our completely safe streets grinned at us as we walked to church. The owner of the town's only café gave us pie after each meal we bought as a kind of *gratis* offering. The school board elected me to offer the invocation at commencement. Wedding gifts poured in ahead of the event. The family doctor who delivered you into this world was proud to counsel you in every regard concerning those matters that country people would not speak of for reasons of propriety.

Our romance was publicized beyond what I had expected or desired. The hoopla was overdone. I became ever more uneasy, still fearing that my own inconsistent definition of "love" and "being in" or "falling in" it had become no clearer.

The lane that formed the driveway to your home was lined with tall trees. Those cedars formed a canopy under which I had promised to marry you. The trees stood erect and had a towering stability that made one feel indecisive. Each night as I took you home, they were witness to my future fears about the night I would no longer take you to your home, but to mine. My home! I didn't have a home! And furthermore, if I somehow were able to build a nest from my modest income, providing was not so great a concern as loving. I wanted all the fulfillment for both of us that our union would bring, but chastened my mind for daring to marry without the certainty of "in-love-ness." The day approached.

Each year the chamber of commerce of our little town set forth the eligible young women of the hamlet in a penny-voting tradition by which one of them would be elected as the town queen. Even though we were engaged, your popularity in the community made it inevitable that you would be the town's choice.

On the night of the coronation, the community was jubilant. You were the people's choice as you had been mine. I was proud, for even as your youthful attendants scurried about you, everyone knew that you were promised to the young minister who, as part of the audience, surveyed the coronation.

I had dressed formally to match the occasion, and when the festivities were over, we drove home, still jubilant. Now, when I look at those old photos, I realize your gown was a style popular to that day, but now uncommon and quaint. Still, that night a regal aura settled upon you under the dainty rhinestone tiara. To view you on that occasion was to want to rush quickly into marriage—not because I was settled about the issue of love, but because I really wanted you.

My patience with being engaged was growing threadbare. But this was a proper community and things had to be done properly and in good time. The time was May—a proper time—printed in the engravings. I was the proper person, a proper bachelor who ministered in an acceptable way. You were the proper bride, acceptable to the circle of fussbudget women who gave you a bridal shower and loaded you with monogrammed sheets, towels, pillowslips, and silver. The china they gave you was as proper as the white Bible they gave you to carry in the wedding.

"It has to be done right," insisted the older women who had guarded the social life of the church and community since the first houses had been built. Some of the ranchers were opposed to the things the farmers suggested. The musical *Oklahoma* had suggested that the ranchers and the farmers should be friends, but they often found social reasons to disagree over propriety.

The elopement rumor seemed increasingly more attractive, I decided. Increasingly, I grew impatient for the folderol to end. I was ever more eager, therefore, to be married. The weeks crawled by.

The wheat grew tall, and the light green heads beckoned us to view the fields. Nature had ever been the place for love. At weary last, the grain began to turn a lusty gold. Mid-May had come, and the sweet smell of harvest colored my senses and made me wish the last burdensome weeks were out of the way.

We flew to the fields with a picnic basket and a thermos of tea. I kissed you as we lay in the sun. Our kisses were but the gates of whatever walled and waiting experiences would come beyond the lagging ceremony.

The same sun that saw our grandparents come to the good land looked down on us that afternoon.

"The sun is good," I said.

"Do you love me with all your heart?" you asked.

"As I can know what love is," I replied.

You never pressed me for any contrived reply. You changed the subject. "Are you ready for the honeymoon?"

"Yes—after propriety," I complained.

We kissed and loaded all the paraphernalia back into the car.

The week came to an end.

Propriety grew to fervor. Friends arrived, the church was decorated with satin bows and long candles.

"We've had a lot of reverends since this county was settled and this church was built," said one of the women of the parish, "but you're the first to marry in it. I cleaned the windows and waxed the pews myself."

What was an honor to them was a horror to me. I remember that the night before the wedding, I drove you home. The bachelor's party had been an occasion of boredom and sweetmeats. At least the months of waiting were over.

That night I opened your car door and let you out. The grain was early-ripened and nearly gold. The harvest moon came early through the gray-green boughs of the tall cedars. I kissed you for the final time before the ceremony, still wanting ahead of time what could only come when the time was proper.

"I love you," you said again, and you meant it.

I was quiet, treasuring your words without reply.

A SILENT HUNGER

My love must wait. Still, there's an appetite
That drives me to the tasting of that fruit
That never should be picked so green. The night
Stirs my desire and summons up a brute
That's always ravenous when he awakes.
No logic quiets him. No piety
Can make the bruin rest. His fire forsakes
All love and feeds on frothing chemistry.
How well you wait; avoid the hurried slur
Of love that can't forgo her meal one day.
Temperance alone waits best—prefers
The total soul, thus orders need away.
When love contrives the whole, then love is good.
And hurried need reduces love to food.

7

$\mathscr{B}$ELATED $\mathscr{A}$FFIRMATION

It was a May wedding. Country men in plain but sturdy suits brought their women. The congregation who had gathered in increasing numbers over my three years of ministry had swollen to a crowd such as the church had rarely seen. The waiting was over. Still the inner question lingered: what did it mean to be "in love"?

During our engagement, I had sifted my tentative logic again and again. I had managed the honesty of separating love into two facets: platonic and selfish. The platonic commitments were visible. Eros was always love in business for itself. Marriage commitment was structured and elitist in its ceremonial declaration. It was noble and clean and altruistic. Beyond the high white altar, however, waited the other kind of love—impatient, fiery, and immediate. Eros was the "honeymoon," a kind of greedy intimacy that left its high-sounding pledges and made starving demands. Altar love wore tuxedos and promised endurance regardless of health, wealth, or death. It eulogized by candlelight such things as character, idealism, God, the home, and eternity.

The problem was that both kinds of love were still too much one category for me. My thoughts mixed altruism and desire till they were tangled and twisted together. My noblest promises ended in serving only myself. When I became honest, desire loomed large with me, while altruism occupied your own thoughts during our engagement.

You wanted to give, "for better, for worse, forever . . . till death do us part . . . in sickness and in health." On the other hand, I too much wanted the getting.

I begged your forgiveness of my weaker egocentric definitions of love. I was unsure, and yet I craved the same certainty you displayed. I've heard it said that men crave sex yet call it love, while women idealize love beyond such hungry definitions. It seemed to me a remote proposition that *eros* could ever bring me to the utter self-sacrifice I promised at the altar.

In the weeks just prior to the wedding, a new issue began to occupy my mind: integrity—honor in search of the best reputation. If one could not know the surety of "being in love," one could at least tell the truth. The words of Richard Lovelace in *Lucasta, Going to the Wars,* resurfaced in my memory: "I could not love thee dear so much, loved I not honor more."

I knew that if I ever had a chance to be "in love," it could only lie in the formal promises of the wedding, for those vows were based on integrity. Real love had to be built on honor and not appetite.

Jewish marriages were made secure by this very

principle. When people made altar promises, they kept them, and promises were made to be kept, especially altar promises. This principle made the child-marriage vows of the European feudal system sometimes result in happy marriages and always in stable marriages.

In the midst of my unresolved inner quarrels over the nature of love, the day came. The church was filled to overflowing by two o'clock. Everyone was on time except the parson. I stood there fidgeting, angry that the preacher had abandoned us, and while I waited, one of the groomsmen, in an effort to ease my nerves, offered a kind of busy chitchat. He turned to me and said, "It must be wonderful to be in love."

"It must be," I replied. He detected the uncertainty in my reply.

"What? Are you not in love?" he asked. His tuxedo made him look more like my formal judge than my personal friend.

"I can't say for sure," I replied.

"If you don't know for sure that you are in love, you ought to march in there right now and call this whole thing off!"

I looked at the crowd. His logic seemed sound. Anybody would have agreed with him. The whole world was married on the basis of having fallen in love. Still, I looked at the crowd in fear. I felt green at his terrifying suggestion.

"No," I said, "I will not call it off. I will, rather, stand there at the altar, where I have so often preached the truth, and once more speak in truth. Honor precedes love and everything good is rooted in integrity." He looked puzzled that I could suddenly be such a practical philosopher in what to him seemed the shadow of the guillotine. His jaw dropped open in unbelief and his long chin crushed his dicky and tie. My logic was clearly an unsure way to him. In a while the parson arrived, and we spoke the formal words and made the legal promises, all with integrity, as I had planned.

The aisles soon filled with reception lines, and a gallery of photos was born in a thousand flash bulb explosions. It was over in a fatiguing four hours, and at last we climbed gratefully into our car and drove off for the honeymoon. How odd it felt suddenly to realize that I didn't have to take you home—at least not to your home—but to mine. I was imprisoned in an odd sensation that all my wrangling was useless. We were married. Love was now defined. And yet marriage was like taking you on a date, only it wasn't a date—or at least it was a legal, postmarriage date. The odd sensation hit me that we were both very right and very wrong at the same time.

I felt sheepish when we arrived at last at the motel, a hundred miles away. I felt like I needed to show my I.D. so the clerk would understand. We checked in. The man behind the desk noticed our car outside with "Just Married" stenciled on it in shoe polish calligraphy. He gave us our room key and smiled oddly at me. I wondered if he had ever been "in love" and what right he felt he had to grin the way he did. I needed neither his permission nor his encouragement.

From that night, the months flew by. The fields yielded up their grain. Finally the sod itself was turned over to become furrowed fields ready for the new planting and thus the next harvest.

We found, through an unusual channel of ministry, a new and interim position a long way from the rural church I had resigned. We moved from Oklahoma to Iowa in winter. It was our first time to live outside of Oklahoma, and we discovered winter in a new way. More than winter, we discovered the romance of winter. The snow came frequently and piled up in great walls along every road. By general agreement, that winter was the worst ever. Even the older Iowans said it had snowed more than they could remember. But we were enchanted with the Iowa winter.

There was always a newness in the snow and nothing so shuts out the world as the white silence that buries all commerce in formal sanctity. Most of those we knew avoided the storms, but we relished them. The best way to see a snowflake is on an eyelash. So what others watched through windowpanes we saw close at hand.

Walking in the magic, I suddenly felt alive. I was struck by a strange emotion, a new exhilaration. I watched a snowflake catch a curl of your auburn hair and stick in obstinacy. You laughed and the cold drew a clear, pure sound into your laughter.

"This is it!" I cried. "Now I love you—all at

once!" I stopped and drew you up to me and we embraced in the falling glory. At once I knew who you were and who I was. I knew how honor comes ahead of all. Integrity I had offered on a May day in Oklahoma, and love had come in its own time in the snowy enchantment of Iowa. As for me, I was the same, yet not the same. I was "in love," yet still "in honor." I knew that when honor precedes everything, everything is right—and in the rightness, love is free to find itself.

In the powerful exaltation of a new declaration, we stopped beneath a lonely lamp post. The flakes flew furiously about us and shut the world away. "I love you," I said softly. The silence of the night folded us into a new oneness. I kissed you.

WINTER LOVE

When first I saw the distant winter sun
Set gently free the auburn in your hair
With softer light, I knew I had begun
To understand the depth of our affair.
The country church in summer held our rite,
Some "legal" pledge that droned a legal love
I could not mean, until that crystal night
I stooped to kiss a snowflake from your glove.
It's strange December would confirm the vows
We made in May. Nor could I really know
The promise stood, till in the chill somehow
It came to me. I held you in the snow.
What summer but conceived, the cold allowed
To be, and winter-nourished love will grow.

8

$\mathcal{N}$EBRASKA

My seminary studies ended as did the interim position in the Iowa congregation. I was ready at last to assume the pastorate of my first "full-time church." The church was in a river town of Eastern Nebraska. I remember how frightened we were. I was afraid the congregation wouldn't like me, though I was all but sure they would adore you. I remember my curious sense of destiny as I prepared to drive into the state for the first time. The state line was the meandering Missouri River, and I actually felt excited as we drove onto the bridge that spanned it.

My great-grandparents had crossed this very river in covered wagons before the bridges were built. My grandmother had been born in the plains west of the Missouri River on the trek west. Her parents had even named her Sadie Nebraska. I felt exhilarated to realize my great grandparents had been to this very river a scant seventy years before me. Their love for the frontier overcame me for a moment. I felt a strange sensation of homecoming. "Just think," I said, "the old Mormon trail passed right through here. Brigham Young's 'handcarters' crossed the river just north of here and wintered on the Omaha side of the river." But you seemed untouched by my historical enthusiasm. Your practical side always retreated from my naive excitement.

We drove across the silver-brown river. Above it was an old trestle. Every rivet in the steel bridge was rusted, and the drab iron was laced together with orange freckles that bled in rusty stripes.

It was a moment of sunlight and new beginnings. The genesis was mine. I faced across the river with two loves. I loved Christ in whose name I went to serve the Nebraskans. I loved you as well for your willingness to become one with those I went to serve. Before the car droned to a stop, a gaudy cock pheasant, in the act of displaying his colors for sumer, bolted into the red sky like a prairie comet. I was content.

"This is the land of William Jennings Bryan," I said.

"And Willa Cather and Mari Sandoz," you added.

"The Union Pacific starts in Omaha," I said.

You asked where it ended. "At the ocean," I said, letting you know I had no idea. After all, it didn't matter where the railroad ended, it was enough to know that it began in Nebraska.

The rusty-rivet bridge delivered us safely to the land new to us, yet not to our forebears.

Though we had never been to the state before, we felt instantly at home. The parsonage came alive with activity. We had boxes and boxes of belongings. The house was not ours and yet your own personal touches proclaimed it so. You took a small house built by somebody else, for somebody else, and you made it ours. There were raspberry bushes and fruit trees in the back and a respectably green lawn in the front. We weren't exactly homesteaders, but we were convinced that we belonged.

The congregation was small—a composition of warm folks who knew God and the land. There were few "old timers" in the congregation, and thus I felt much less romance than I thought I would feel. Most of the younger folk, like us, had also discovered the state by crossing the Missouri.

Before the end of our first month in the little river town, a square block in the business district caught fire and burned. The Historic Hotel was destroyed, and much of the city's quaint charm perished with it. Before the end of our first year, the thawing of spring snows changed the Missouri from a river into an ochre ocean and our small city into a brown Venice of angry waterways. Valuable farmland was destroyed along with many of the homes in the city and its environs. The flood receded. Summer came.

We decided to drive west and see the rise in the plains and great dome of the western skies. The night skies intrigued us most. We had never seen the stars as we came to know them in Nebraska. They defied their light-year definitions and seemed to hang just above the prairies.

Winter on the plains can be vicious, but Iowa had made us ready. We learned to love Nebraska's winters even more than her summers. The silence of

a great white storm, the fireplaces and teakettles and
hot bread, formed the ecstasy of our January commu-
nion. I revelled in Whittier's delightful prophecy:

> *The sun that brief December day*
> *Rose cheerless over hills of grey,*
> *And, darkly circled, gave at noon*
> *A sadder light than waning moon.*
> *Slow tracing down the thickening sky*
> *Its mute and ominous prophecy—*

And suddenly, we would be "Snowbound."

When the storms were most furious, we most
loved them. Robert W. Service in *The Spell of the
Yukon* spoke for both of us when he wrote of that
place in winter. He spoke of the "strong life that
never knows harness." He exulted in Canada's winters, and we applied his song to ourselves from January to January:

> *The winter! the brightness that blinds you,*
> *The white land locked tight as a drum,*
> *The cold fear that follows and finds you,*
> *The silence that bludgeons you dumb.*
> *The snows that are older than history,*
> *The woods where the weird shadows slant;*
> *The stillness, the moonlight, the mystery,*
> *I've bade 'em good-bye—but I can't.*

I had never believed that those who served
Christ should "sanctify their geography." Only people are sacred and beloved of God, not places. God
prefers no province above another. Yet, for me, God
had given us this place, and the place was good.

I bought a shotgun that first year and became a hunter. I was never a good hunter, though in time my skill improved. But hunting was nature, and nature was the prairies teeming with life. How I loved the russet fields, studded with snow and the sound of my own boots crunching across a sea of white listening for the crow of a cock pheasant on a clean winter morning. The mackinaw I wore and the thermos of hot coffee made me ever more certain that God had ordained this province for me: this gold was mine! Here, where the Platte River meandered across the plains, frozen and still, I walked and rehearsed God's goodness. Long before me, my kinsmen had walked the wide, generous banks of this same frozen river.

I could see why the Hebrews first found God in the light of the stars and in the sighing winds. The field became for me His dwelling place. Not only did He pervade the streams and the fields, but He seemed present in the very lives of the people in our parish. They were the real dwelling place of the Divine Savior, who met with us each time we met with them.

Do you remember the old man, whose face was raw-red from seventy winters on his farm? He and "his woman" were alive with the life-force of breaking sod for half a century of springtimes in the plains. They had married in 1913, and he had followed a shining plow share that cut a black furrow, fifty years long. For the first twenty-five years, he had followed his great Clydesdales, and for the last twenty-five, he had driven a gasoline tractor. And best of all, they were patient with my naiveté. They were alive with the resonance of living on the land, and their quiet dynamism surged through their quaint simplicity. They had seen God in a thousand prairie storms, yet listened patiently as I described Him—often weakly—in my sermons.

How much they taught us about life on the plains. From them we learned how to use the autumn to store the fruit of summer. The old woman's gnarled hands were strong with the seriousness of her task. They dipped into the steaming cauldrons of glass jars a delicious security against the winter. We learned to eat in February what we canned in August.

The old man finally grew faint with cancer. We watched a firm frame that never yielded to the harsh life of the plains lose a wretched battle with an ugly inner enemy. I wanted so to help him win against the foe that fought too hard. I held the giant hand that once had managed the handles of the wooden plow. I prayed for him, desirous that the God whom he once absorbed through the very soles of his leather boots from the brown earth of Nebraska would heal him. It was no use. The enemy was great. The old man died. I put my arm around his new widow who, after sixty years of marriage, could only say that from Nebraska to heaven was not a long distance.

There were others like these two. Others whose passing left us all the more alone and yet fulfilled.

The land was ours—as they were. I wanted to touch, feel, and belong to the land as they did. I wanted to see Christ in a kind of primeval splendor, like sunrise in Eden. I never drove through the green plains at daybreak except that I said of the state, in the words of Eleanor Farjeon: "Morning has broken like the first morning." Or the first verse of the *Te Deum Laudamus:*

> *We praise thee, O God.*
> *We acknowledge thee to be the Lord.*
> *All the earth doth worship thee.*

It was a good land—and good to us. In December of our first winter there, I placed my hand on you and felt the movement of new life. I knew the baby would come in the middle of the furious winter. But I also knew it would be all right. It had to be! Our love would have all that it could desire: the land, the people, ourselves, and a child—a son or daughter. The child would be born less than a hundred miles and a hundred years from where a nameless midwife brought my grandmother into this world. We were home. Our unborn baby moved beneath my hand and you smiled.

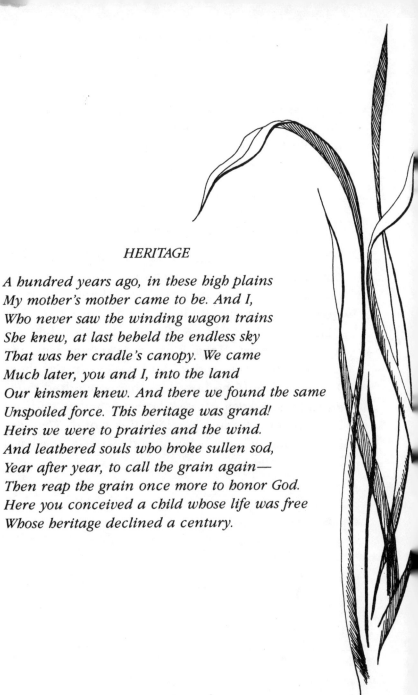

HERITAGE

A hundred years ago, in these high plains
My mother's mother came to be. And I,
Who never saw the winding wagon trains
She knew, at last beheld the endless sky
That was her cradle's canopy. We came
Much later, you and I, into the land
Our kinsmen knew. And there we found the same
Unspoiled force. This heritage was grand!
Heirs we were to prairies and the wind.
And leathered souls who broke sullen sod,
Year after year, to call the grain again—
Then reap the grain once more to honor God.
Here you conceived a child whose life was free
Whose heritage declined a century.

9
THE _CUBS_

They came to us from God and from our own promises to each other. Before they came, the waiting
came: the swelling of your womanhood, the grand
grotesqueness, the obtuse excellence. We cheered
impatiently and waited twice. Like others we observed around us in the church, we feared the lagging days would disappoint us. We trembled lest our
children should come as things born in horror. Twice
our fears proved groundless.

Our daughter arrived in February, and our son
on a balmy night in summer a year and a half later.
They were born a little close together and their closeness made them seem like twins. The care that they
required left us sometimes tired in the unceasing demands of their infancy. But they grew. Before long,
they were alive with themselves, and the world they
discovered was filled with sunshine and snow, all
created just for them.

The days seemed to tumble over each other as
they played, like young cubs in a Disney nature film.
Our love was endorsed by our delight in them and
our unwillingness to ever see them suffer because of

any unsteadiness in our own relationship. We came to understand that their security came so much from our togetherness.

Our youngest especially needed us. He suffered several seasons of pneumonia in his infancy, and each attack left him weak. We were always afraid that his convalescence would be too slow to allow him to regain the stamina he needed before his next attack of illness came.

But when his first winter was gone, he seemed well enough, and we decided we would take the children camping. We were never good campers, and yet our parish offered us such a small salary that other kinds of vacation outings were unaffordable.

How nice it was, and how splendid the mountains were. I remember how you cheerfully warmed the children's milk by the open fire that blazed before the little tent we had borrowed for the outing. We traveled in the Rockies, which were only a few hundred miles from home and which provided us with new vistas for our relationship.

Camping intimidated us at first. We were afraid that the bears would rob our picnic baskets. It was an unfounded phobia that gave way to the more real danger that our own cubs would steal all they could nibble while our backs were turned! I remember the simple joy of the four of us zipped into one sleeping bag. We were lovers—a family of lovers. Our combined togetherness with the children was sleeping-bag cozy, and our little ones became the warm completion of ourselves.

They grew. Every year before they started to school, they welcomed our annual trip to the mountains as did we. I remembered all my mother had taught me of real abundance, and now I tried to teach it to them. We let them know how rich we all were. They were so well off that they never seemed to notice how we bypassed the swank motels, opting for life under the blue sky and borrowed canvas.

It was our wealthy poverty that taught us first to love long walks on shaded trails. And the children, too, enjoyed the sun and the trees. I remember a night in Wyoming, when we were snuggled into fleecy sleeping bags. We turned on the radio just before falling asleep and heard a static and nasal, electronic voice tell us that some bears had mauled a family of campers in Wyoming that very afternoon. We suddenly became afraid. We were terrorized by an image of a vicious animal ripping its way into our tent.

We looked at each other and then at the cubs. We spoke in whispers as to what course of action we should take if real bears came. I went to the car and took out our camping ax. I felt nervous and looked at the ax doubtfully. I wondered how either of us would really fare at axing bears.

The darkness closed in tightly when I extinguished the battery lantern. We listened for a crashing and lumbering form among the timbers. The darkness of the night grew thick and our eyes were as useless as they were eager to help. Our ears listened and informed our minds. Our minds were the real enemies, constructing images that kept us awake. The images were horrible—yellow leathery lips, fangs and claws and terror.

Gradually the hours passed, and the fresh light of morning seemed to wake the alien forest with a new friendliness. Our fatigue overcame us and our taut bodies eased into rest. We dozed just as the sun was becoming intense. The children stirred, then were awake at once, clamoring for playclothes and tennis shoes and a chance to run.

Happily, as I look back, I see that most of the time our protective instinct was not trapped in dread such as this. Still, their welfare made the days anxious. The little one always had a fever, and the older, a special reason for concern. Both of them required minor hospitalizations and extra care.

There were simple things that kept their common necessity in mind. Once we lost our son at Disneyland. And our daughter once suffered an injury and a concussion that was to require a long hospitalization and a siege of plastic surgery to correct.

But in the process of their growing, we learned and grew, too. During their teen years, our means improved. We learned how close a family could grow while traveling in a small European car across the Swiss Alps or the Rhine Valley or the rolling hills of Cornwall. In foreign climates, we were forced to use good, simple English and to talk to each other as we traveled. Our rented auto became a womb of live communication. We talked to each other in lands where we knew too little of the local tongue to talk to anyone else.

I loved you as you loved the children and myself. I loved you for being unafraid to drive those left-handed cars on the highways of England. I loved you because you made the children secure when they felt menaced and alone in Mexico. I loved you for chiding me when I was too protective of them both. I remember my uneasiness that you quieted so that I could watch our son race to the top of the Teotihuacan Pyramids.

Best of all, I remember how calm you were in every crisis. I was often tense with anxiety until I knew they were safe and the crisis was over.

The days ran past each other, and at last the cubs were taller than us. "Sunrise, sunset. . . ." And soon we all were older and yet made one by the fleeting years. There is a joyful sadness in those years we see now in the photo album. But yesterdays are wistful only because they cannot be called back. We're glad their footprints grew. We knew one day that we would watch them step across the threshold, that the door would swing outward and then shut, echoing with reverberations only our ears would hear.

THE CUBS

The cubs are come! The den is home. See how
They romp. Their noise is contribution to
Our simple joy this present hour. For now
They're cubs. And now we celebrate the two
Of them that are of us. The summer's fair,
The woods are warm with sun. Dance, little ones.
And play for us to warm our little lair
Before the forest hides from distant suns.
What shall the future hold for you? What pain
May come with autumn's frost? The woods may grow
Quite barren and all the sunny fields know rain.
Your play could know the killing blight of snow.
Play in the sun, for no day comes again,
Time feeds upon our youth and leaves us men.

10

A WIDER LOVE

The church of rural Nebraska was soon replaced by the one in the city. Here was our new work in the only large city that Nebraska knew. The new church called for more industry and required so much time that much of the romance I had felt in the early church was lost.

The congregation grew, and its very demands seemed to rise against our relationship. A decade of years proclaimed a growing agenda. We had once claimed Nebraska like conquistadors, but were all too soon discovering that her beautiful people had turned from being the possessed to being the possessors. Unlike the rural church, the city church grew so rapidly that its few members soon numbered more than two thousand, and still they came.

It was not until we got to the city that I struggled so with the problem of pain. Why it should have begun then, I cannot say. Perhaps I walked less in the country and took less time to know the outdoors Christ, who was complete in Himself in His nature. Perhaps my own process of aging made me suddenly aware of those who had to face great ordeals of suffering in which the God of mercy seemed so often deaf to all their needs.

Even if we had no real answer for pain, at least we had compassion. The church became a haven for the hurting, and we both sought ways to extend the sovereignty of the Savior until He who had caused us to love each other should extend His love for others through us. As the smaller church had its special reminiscences, so did the large one.

We both loved Anne, whose charm and wit had made her instantly the sweetheart of the church. Then came cancer. Anne turned to us, and we turned to Him. Eagerly we besought Him to help her win her battle with that disease that all her charm and wit could not forestall.

Her dying hurt us because we could not staunch the hurt that it caused her. It wasn't just that we lost a friend to death, but that the dying so dehumanized that friend, that we lost her long before we really lost her. It was hard indeed for us to understand the horror of what had happened to Anne. Why did God allow such a brilliant woman to become the sallow, empty-eyed thing that now lived in the same place her bright personality had once resided?

Anne was but one.

There was also Bill, a tall Nebraskan, whose excitement in life was blunted by a dull prophecy from his doctor. He, too, died in tubes, strung up in all the rubberized paraphernalia that prolonged his physiology, but not his life.

I was with him when he died, and he made me

promise to care for his widow until she could find work, for the disease had claimed their livelihood and left their family penniless.

I made promises to him . . . to them . . . to all of them. Each of them needed my time. Funerals were not so frequent in the city, for most of the families were young. But the helpless loneliness of those who had to watch as death invaded their families grieved me and demanded more and more of my stamina.

I found that no serious issue could be answered quickly. I remember the horror of Bucky, who was killed by a speeding car. Here I wrangled once again with God. Why was a little boy in our congregation impaled on the spike of a Buick hood ornament? Bucky's family took months for the healing. So did Ricky's parents. Ricky was another child with a congenital heart ailment that claimed his life on the operating table. More and more people brought problems to our congregation which we could not pray away.

They loved us as much as they seemed to need us. Perhaps they loved us *because* they needed us. Here was a part of our difficulty with the parish. You felt they needed *me*, and I felt they needed *us*. It was your continuing sense of prayer as a way of life that was the motivation for my life of prayer.

I never loved you more than when you shared our personal time with those we served. There were times when I knew you resented the congregation for taking advantage of our time. How many hundreds of calls interrupted the very special meals that you had labored so hard to prepare, knowing that the preparation would delight me? Yet the meals grew cold and their delicacy faded on the plates as our evenings were taken away by urgent pleas.

We have always reacted differently to need. I found tears a way of response. I confess that crying never seemed a manly quality, but sometimes a maudlin mood would take control of my emotions. By contrast, you were a strong example of emotional consistency. You laughed more readily and freely than I. Naturally the congregation loved you, but I could tell in your strong silence that you felt incidental in our marriage because of their needs, which more and more came between us.

I could see what they were doing to us, but I found myself unable to stop loving them, even as I would have been unable to stop loving you. You were my dearest love, but I could not forsake all I felt for them. My ardor for both you and them was hidden in a principle that had grown with me across the years. I knew Christ loved all, and I was not at liberty to despise anyone that He loved. It was in no sense a negative principle, however. I loved because He loved—not as intensely, but just as certainly.

When I would see you caught in the fatigue of the endless stream of people who came through our home, I loved you for a second reason: your generous offering of yourself to the Nebraskans. There was ever a note of cheer in your demeanor. The tea was always hot, and the lemon and honey were always near at hand. The best thing about your hospitality was that it was generous and instant. You were a woman whose love was visible in all your hand extended.

Eyes welcome friends before words do, and no one who ever saw your eyes could doubt that you also loved life. Thus, we were one in all we loved. How safe all romance is when Christ's love precedes it. There were times when you might have been impatient or short with me, but you remembered how He loved both me and those I served. I wanted not to love them, for they stole our lives with their urgent issues and all too often took up too much of the time we craved for ourselves.

I remember a horrible Friday when I had a funeral in the afternoon and a wedding rehearsal in the evening. The next morning was a second funeral with an afternoon wedding. I remember the emotional portages that swept me between grief and joy as event followed hard upon dissimiliar event. One hour I was ministering to those in despair—the next hour was characterized by bright hope.

I can think of specific people who have taken my time and, thus, yours. None required more time than a talented artisan who had never learned to read. I wanted to teach him. I began to meet with him regularly and to introduce him to letters and words. Week by week, my frustrations increased as my reluctant disciple learned slowly the simple glory of

English. I used to think in my restlessness, "Why doesn't he learn faster so I can get home to you earlier?"

I felt like Higgins in *Pygmalion*. How hard it was to hurry a grown man to syllable recognition. For one year, I taught my friend—we moved from simple children's classics to the New Testament—and by the end of the year, he had learned to read. But we were one year older and the lost year was unrenewable.

I am sorry that I did not handle church urgencies in a more balanced fashion. I loved you both: the church was His body, and you, the very extension of myself. I was unable to resist or renounce either. But how could I affirm both lovers and yet keep honestly the ardor of both of my romantic affairs?

How often from Valentine's Day to Valentine's Day did we celebrate our love by reading Elizabeth Barrett Browning's *Sonnets from the Portuguese?* Her ever-popular Sonnet 43 was our favorite:

> *How do I love thee? Let me count the ways.*
> *I love thee to the depth and breadth and height.*
> *My soul can reach, when feeling out of sight*
> *For the ends of beings and ideal grace.*

And we found our own maturing confession in her final lines:

> *I love thee with the breath,*
> *Smiles, tears, of all my life!—and, if God choose,*
> *I shall but love thee better after death.*

Elizabeth Barrett Browning spoke for us both. And here at last, loved deeply, I also loved beyond the boundaries of our relationship and was delighted that you understood. In loving all those whom Christ called me to love, you sometimes waited in the wings. Yet yours was an active wait—you loved them too, and we rejoiced that Christ had called us both to love more widely than ourselves.

DEBT

I love you, church. You wear an empty face,
Yet His and yours are one. If love can be,
Here's what I give to you. Here are the ways
I love. I love you as He loved the sea
Whereon He walked—as eagles love the sky.
I love you with an eager joy born twice
Or as a goodly merchant who would buy
Though it cost all—the pearl of greatest price.
I love you as a prisoner set free.
I love you as a treasure in a field.
I love you as I prize Gethsemane,
Where brother-love bled rich and hate was sealed.
As steel can maul a hand—and make men new—
I have been loved and therefore I love you.

11

$\mathscr{R}$EPENTANCE

When lovers ask forgiveness, their repentance is a rare and haunting brokenness.

Magdalenes sin openly and answer for their deeds at public executions. But marital transgressions are seldom blatant; they carry a quiet guilt before the stern but mute tribunals of the soul.

Marriages rarely die in blazing flames of infidelity. They die from lack of care. I always promised myself I would not take for granted that which I prized so dear.

I never wronged you in great ways. My sins were little transgressions. But each became thin sinews in a growing web of pain. And each of them was committed always in the name of ministry to someone else in need. You served them by gently forgiving me for all the promises I made to you and broke. I sinned by accepting your ready forgiveness and later by expecting it.

If I needed to be five minutes late for dinner, I knew you wouldn't question it. If I were caught stealing time from you to give to the congregation, I knew you wouldn't mind. I came home so often fatigued from caring outside the parsonage, that I was too tired to care inside.

Then there were the grand hurts. In the ninth year of our marriage, your mother died. You were forced to watch her atrophy in the pain of an incurable degeneration. She required so much of your love and yet I confess now my own lack of support. I had by this time cared for so many with cancer in the church that my eyes were blinded by my own familiarity with death. A thousand times I have wished I could turn back the clock and touch you when your bright eyes were made dead by fear and fatigue. I lived with you without shedding a single tear to confirm that you did not grieve alone. How shall I say I'm sorry?

The years were far too furious for me to count, and losing count, I ran too fast. From New Year's Eve to New Year's Eve, we gathered at the clock and toasted the loud chimes that ate at us day by day with such a hassled agenda that we could not measure our days nor even catch the import of their furious demands. Besides the cares of the congregation, I set goals for myself designed to push my own career along. I wrote and published, and all I wrote, you typed a thousand times—never of necessity, but with joy.

I am lost to remember all the savage nights I drove us to the finishing of some manuscript. In the wee small hours of morning, while the children slept, we spoke in the darkness, of my career, of some deadline or hurried goal. Yet never did you castigate me for the dreams I wanted to achieve.

How glorious was your celebration of my life! Your love served the typing table as a kind of altar where you were high priestess in love with me and all my dreams. Your only weakness was your lack of critical judgment—you loved all I did and grew angry with my critics, even when they were right. You loved with faith that believed you would one day be married to a writer. How did you justify keeping your faith fettered to me? Did you even consider the price it cost your hope of career just to believe in me so much?

I think not.

For you were angrier than I when a rejected manuscript came back again.

I wondered that you never wanted life a little more for yourself. I remember reading you a passage by a certain woman psychologist who felt that women of real stature should have their own goals and not identify too closely with the goals and dreams of their husbands. She called the serving wife a "limited success woman." It seemed a slur from which I wanted to deliver you. Yet the statement indicted me more than you. At such moments of truth, I confessed my selfishness to God and to you. But you insisted that my life and yours were exactly what you wanted for yourself.

For a long time, the idea distressed me. I tried to get you to seek your own career—to take up some diversion or hobby or social circle with other women. Still you desired to lose your ambition in the service of my own. The more I encouraged you to seek your own career, the more you moved into mine. Such wholesale endorsement of my dreams made it all too easy to take advantage of you. Without realizing it, I began to take your willful submergence of your own needs into my life as normal to a marriage relationship.

For fifteen years, you worked as a secretary in the city because without your salary we could not survive. Our church was too small to pay us anything more than subsistence. Yet your salary was never a contested contribution to our funds. It was always as much mine as yours. It was not that I tore it from you, you always gave it to me without the slightest possessiveness. I took it for "our" account.

Here was another of my blunders. You were content in every state of substance or need. What you had was enough. I was the materialist—the malcontent—particularly in early marriage. I ever needed so much more than you. Without grumbling, you seemed to fancy what I fancied, to crave what I craved, to need what I saw as needful.

How you scrimped from this or that to be sure that the groceries were adequate or that the children had mittens in the winter. The car had to run so I could serve the people. Against the grocery fund or the clothing fund, I waged a practical war. Spark plugs for the car seemed more important to me than mittens or galoshes for the children.

What bothers me now, as I reconsider these years, is that I felt my priorities were *the* priorities.

But it was not only the material crisis I resented.

How I wish I could have given more than I did of myself. My stamina ever seemed greater than yours. I required less sleep and could hurry the days and yet warm the long hours of night with my desk lamp. Every day was pushed by a thousand different ideas to yield up every minute for my goals. Every season of the year was made to serve. This was especially true of winter. While the snow stacked silently outside my study window, I read on into the night— night after night. Perhaps this extra reading time was why I always loved winter best of all. But while I steeped my mind in the winter storms at your expense, you were always down the hall typing until your stamina was spent. Two or three A.M. would ever come upon us like married celibates pushing the hours for product. When the children cried, the clatter of your typewriter would stop while you marched to their bedrooms to be a mother. And when they were quiet, you would come back again. But best of all were those times I heard your footfalls on the oak floor coming in my direction. You would slip in, set a cup of steaming tea by the lamp, and then slip your arms around me.

Why was I so serious? Why could I not more often stop to enjoy your youth? Mechanistically I would greet your query of love by asking how the manuscript was going. You would kiss me and reply—and then ask me where to hyphenate something like *trinitarian* before you went back to your work, leaving me to mine. In early marriage, we walked regularly in the snow, but we hurried the winters as we grew older.

I regret now my lost Februarys. If I could, I would repeat those years and would make each one better serve your sense of self-importance. I would give each church member my fatigue and answer you with freshness. Others would receive the lackluster stamina that was left over after I gave you the day's vitality.

My eye would be brighter for you. My ear would not grow dull of hearing. My attitude would be entire. I would exalt the low, low altar of your need. The days would be so much the more our own— could we come again to younger love.

REPENTANCE

I sipped the cream of our relationship
And glutted on your generosity.
I grasped your bounty—seized with a strangle grip
your free and ever soft gentility.
You called—my ears heard voices far away.
Your face was ever there—I passed it by
And gazed at other faces in the fray.
I loved the distant and the near denied.
What arrogance that public altar vows
Should be so showy when they say, "I do,"
Flashing diamond rings before a crowd
Of exhibitionists, who never knew
That public words, speak for their own applause
And make us strut before our own hurrahs.

12

*T*HE *S*EASON OF *D*ARKNESS

We were married for a dozen years before our trial by fire. It was our sixth year in the city. It pains me even now to recall that winter of our discontent.

It was our year of greatest crisis, and yet the year brought me to an open confession of my need for you and Christ. It was for me a season of double pain, for I was made to look upon twin medusae.

The first trial was a material matter that came in the form of a congregational recommendation that I be dismissed as pastor of the church. The charge was from some older members who felt my leadership was too erratic and impulsive for older folk to follow. My worst fears had to do with finances. I was ill-trained for any other vocation. I knew how to "work for God," as we said in seminary, but I had never held secular employment for any length of time. I sought frantically to find another pulpit, but none was open and my fears of being unable to provide for my family tormented me. For months, the all-powerful chairman of the council continuously pressured me to resign. Most of the others on the council of the church agreed with him. When the critical vote came,

I was saved from this pressure by the congregation itself. The majority of those to whom I ministered stood firmly against the council. I was in the unenviable position of living with a congregation who desired and courageously demanded that I continue, while the board chairman demanded otherwise.

I had never believed that God saw churches in terms of big and little people. How grateful I became that I had ministered to the "little people" in the flock who later stood by us with strength and, through the agonizing months of conflict, were finally able to prevail.

The strain of trying to lead a congregation whose most prominent members did not want me to be the pastor often grew unbearable. I lost much of the joy that I had always felt about my calling. I could, here and there, see little reasons to rejoice, but my inner life grew bleak. Shakespeare's truth characterized my drab view of that whole gloomy time:

> For we, which now behold these present days,
> Have eyes to wonder, but lack tongues to praise.
> (Sonnet 106, lines 13-14)

Month after month, my tension with the council endured, and only after the agony of a church quarrel did it end in rupture and ultimately healing. As it healed, so did I.

There was another medusa I found I could not so easily look upon. To serve Christ is to opt for a kind of social separation that leaves a "man of God" set apart from the more ordinary folks of this world. He who serves God finds that he walks with people, yet alone. The problems can be great, and circumstances can become so furious that they call for steel psyches and a firm pier to endure.

I took the pastorate of the suburban church at the same time and age that a colleague took the pulpit in a neighboring community. Soon after we became pastors and friends, he went blind. His agony sent him into a maelstrom of despair. He purchased a red-tipped cane and went on trying to minster in a black world. He tried to thrust his own handicap aside by the radical giving of himself to others. Our friendship deepened. His need was physical and mine was spiritual. Often I would read to him. His interest in the books I read would send us spiraling away into other fields of discussion.

His blindness set him off on a pilgrimage from hostility to acquiescence to a second sight that reveled in his visionary darkness. His sightlessness revealed a furtive independence. He was eager to reject help and strike out on his own to measure Milton's world of a paradise lost and regained.

The light came to him, and he shared it with me in the year of my greatest despair. "Never love people supremely," he advised me. "Love God before you love his people," he counseled. "For years I served the people of God. I loved the church of God, adored the things of God—now I love only God."

How bright his vision had grown in blackness!

At last I understand why Jesus condemned hypocrisy. It is the enemy of integrity. And that which is the foe of integrity is the enemy of trust. If those who are filled with "God-talk" may act in evil, then is all trust eliminated in the world. If hypocrisy becomes too widespread, no one may be believed and all the saints may be doubted. Then is all the world spoiled. Religion becomes a black affair that only dresses white.

Now my entire ministry was being questioned by one man who spoke of God without the obligation of loving anyone. His popularity seemed unspeakable in light of his hypocrisy.

I felt much like Young Goodman Brown on his way back from the Black Mass. Having seen the archdeacon of Christ burning the black candles at a witches coven, he could never trust his peers again. The first visitor in Gethsemane is always Judas.

Gethsemanes!

William Styron, in *Set This House on Fire,* drew his character Peter Leverett as a man haunted by dreams of betrayal. In one such dream, Leverett sees, outside his rain-streaked window glass, the form of a fiend slinking toward him—menacing him as Hell itself. The harassed hero goes to the phone and dials his one true friend, from whom above all others he would expect help. The phone goes unanswered, ring after ring, till finally the fiend is at his very glass. There through the streaming window pane, he sees the heartless and fanged face of the one true friend he was trying to call.

Betrayed!

Sometimes I named God the culprit of my lost trust in others. How often during my despair, I turned toward you for the final source of strength without which I had no support.

The months dragged by. The snow melted. And spring began to thaw the leafless winter. You met my crisis and gradually turned me from myself. Little by little, my preoccupation with depression subsided, and I came slowly to a newer faith that there was an answer and that it lay in God and men. Trust was possible and believing had to be a part of a healthy future.

Before the crisis, I had been busy and full of "good works." The hospitals, the house calls, shut-ins, and children's programs took all my time. Now I was in need, and I turned in that need to adore you for seeming to need my adoration.

But then I was set to wondering again if I had ever loved you or God. I despised the whole idea of serving either of you as the last resort. I never admire those who turned to God in a crisis. Their Mayday syndrome makes every prayer a plea for help. Their lackluster faith is characterized by a walk of nondevotion when life is easy.

The agony of my desperation made me feel absurd. I never seemed to be able to love both you and God at the same time. When I was deep in prayer or loving Him, I rather tended to be alone with Him. Yet when I emerged from these flights to other worlds, I found a furious need to call for you and to hold you. When my desperation was great, I at last was able to integrate my true loves. I made a vow that I would never again walk with you and God one at a time. We would—the three of us—live life at once in each other's presence.

HYPOCRISY

When I look back, remembering the years,
The very times I stopped to draw you close
To me were times I needed you. My fears
Were giantesque—my menace grandiose.
At other times, I lived away from you,
In lofty towers I climbed alone and prayed.
The flock grew great, my lonely moments few.
The Judas season came. Trust was betrayed.
I tore off several masks to find my face.
I bravely dressed and lied about my fear.
A thin veneer of honor hid disgrace.
You came and made depression talk with cheer.
You were the hand thrust in a lifeless glove
Whose moving finger beckoned me to love.

13

THE NIGHT OF INJURY

It's odd that in the midst of hurried circumstance, a day may break in blue, then darken and shatter into black. I never will forget the agony of a Sunday in May that ended in our disconsolate crying for each other's hurt. The chairman of the church council had finally become open in his hatred of me and demanded that my resignation be given at once.

I hated that day—despised the very month in which it fell! I thought of life and knew that if I could, I should like to live it over and not repeat the season or the day that drove its blade into our new trust in God's love for us—no matter our adversary. Now it seemed that I must resign as pastor. In our despair we had forgotten the truth we had affirmed only a few months before: pain is a filter that purifies the worst waters to make them sweet enough to drink.

How could we forget? Summer was new. The trees were willowy with inner life. They shot out sparks of buds that soon would make the world explode into lush greenery.

Still, the heavy demand of our adversary brought

a thousand feelings of insecurity about our future. I never will forget your downcast look! His hate had fallen upon us openly and in public. The utter absurdity of his charges that I was inept in my leadership and ability to handle the problems of a growing church had left us unable to reply. I felt ashamed to be accused of maladministration. This accusation implied that I was guilty of something even worse—for he failed to define all that he meant by "poor administration" and it sounded as though he meant embezzlement or some great misuse of church property.

I remember the way your dignity seemed to give you precedence over our accuser. I saw your brown eyes blinded by a sting of having to answer vague congregational charges where the shouts came too furious to hear reason. I tried to reason for you, but my own logic was cut off by my own unreasonable anger. When hate screams loudest, love's best answers are dulled to incoherence.

But the greatest pain did not occur in the church business conference. Rather, it arose during the after-process of sorting through the context of the judgment set against us. Prizing truth, I found my own integrity under fire. My powerful enemy on the council of the church persisted in his demand to have me dismissed as pastor.

It was exactly as we had feared it would be. Our accuser did not so much slur me personally, but stated that neither I nor our family was worthy of the pastorate, because he believed we had been remiss in our leadership. His public outcry had been effective. I had been brought to a point of despair where it seemed to me that I must somehow recapture congregational esteem, or resign. I had to reckon with my accusers, who armed themselves with heavy church artillery set against my "poor pastoral ethics."

The sunny afternoon of the congregational meeting gave way to one of the darkest nights our marriage would ever know. We both wept! I decided that I would no longer try to fight my enemies. They were too many. I sat up trying to compose my resignation, determined that when the next night fell, we would both be free of a church that did not seem to want me to be the pastor.

You interrupted me even before I began to write. I remember that you wanted to pray. Prayer was not new to us, but in my bewilderment, I feared it too late for God to restore us to the pastorate. It seemed we could not survive. Still, we joined hands and knelt beside our bed, just as you had taught the children to do. In some ways, we were children, imploring the Father in heaven to hear us. We prayed, I cannot say how long. Sometimes in our agony of hurt, we would stop and love, and our embrace, though awkward, seemed to say to our Almighty Audience that we intended to love each other and to endure together what must be lived out.

We were children, who prayed for our children. They were asleep in their bedrooms, trusting us to care for them. Did they doubt that our love for them would be able to provide the security they needed to survive the tempest? Did they even know that our day had been torn apart with an anguish that seemed to be everlasting? They believed in us, and we believed in God. Yet He seemed so remote as we wept in the darkness.

The darkness was empty. But empty or not, it was friendly. We touched each other whether or not we touched the Almighty. The darkness made it easier to talk. Sometimes we quit talking to God and just talked to each other.

"Forgive me," I whispered, choking my words to great softness. "I've hurt you . . . given our enemies what they need to prove my unworthiness to be pastor." I had no idea where I would go to find a job to keep us alive after I resigned.

I foundered in the darkness for an answer that would shed light on our dim future.

Life had been reduced to the barest reason to hope. I would surely find a job somewhere else. We might lose the house, but we would get by. Suddenly in the darkness, I knew the reason that floated on the pain. We kissed and the darkness thinned.

"No, no, no!" I cried.

We kissed again.

"Now I know the lesson of this May day." Life had been reduced, and what I thought I needed was separating me from what I knew I needed. Suddenly light broke! "I see my sin—I *have* loved this church too much! It's not the church I love—it's you!"

"But you also love the church!" you protested.

"I do love the church. But not so much that losing it will change anything in our relationship. This single day is blessed . . . it has given me a stick for measuring priorities. No . . . no . . . no, not the church primarily. I love you. Forgive me for acting in this crisis as though I could not live without this church. I can . . . yes, my darling. I can live without anything except Christ and yourself."

The content of our love suddenly overwhelmed me. We kissed again from where we yet knelt beside our bed. Then I drew you to the floor and we lay in the darkness which had now filled itself with a divine presence. "Now I know what Bob meant!" I cried into the darkness.

"Bob?" you asked, trying to grasp the rapid turn of the conversation.

"My blind friend. When he first became blind, he told me that in his darkness he learned that we too much love the things of God and too little love God himself." I saw the error of my all-too-shallow affection.

I got up in the night and went to my study and scratched out my resignation. I spared the black ball-point pen its stingy ink. A few words were enough. No charges were answered, no excuses were rendered, no one was hurt, nothing was attacked. I thanked the church for its kindness and apologized to those who had found my ministry inadequate. I spoke of my love for Christ and my love for you and how this double love was set against circumstances that seemed to say I must preserve the integrity of those loves which were primary.

The darkness gave way to a gray morning. I arrived at the church early. I called a friend of mine in a distant city and informed him of the tangleknot situation that would soon force me to attend the morning services and to sever myself from those I had loved but could no longer serve.

He was stunned.

"Perhaps you should resign," he said. "Still, your life speaks clearly of Christ. If you leave the church now in the hurt of all the charges brought against you, you will remember only the pain of separation. Too many good things have happened. Why don't you be open and tell them how you feel and how you are not resigning because you really want to, but because you do not want to embarrass them. Tell them you will not be judged by one man and his council—rather the whole church must speak. For years now, you have tried to preach what it means to be the people of Christ. Now put your life and word to the test! If you have an authentic work of Christ, then it is time to ask them point-blank to demonstrate the love and mercy that you have exalted. If they cannot live and think in terms of the love of Christ for both you and your wife, then you have really failed as a pastor. It is not a church at all if it knows so little of mercy—at least not a church of Christ!"

Suddenly, it occurred to me that perhaps the congregation *was* on our side. In fact, there was a distinct possibility that most of the church council was on our side as well. How did I really know that the council agreed with its autocratic chairman?

In the agony of trying to decide whether or not

to resign, I called a special meeting of the council that afternoon. I appealed for evidence that I had been a maladministrator or had ever misled the church. It felt odd to speak so loudly in my own defense. In confronting the charges brought against me, I felt too much like the aggressor, but most of those present seemed to interpret my defense of myself as a courageous act against a tyrannical leader who, I began to discover, was not so loved as I had supposed. As I had expected, the council chairman was unyielding. He stated firmly that I was guilty. My protest he saw as a clear sign "from the Lord" that my ministry needed to be replaced by a minister who could do it better and with more "honesty." He still would not answer how he felt that I had been dishonest.

We were at an impasse. The atmosphere was lava-hot. Realizing how little Christ's love was being shown by anyone, I was prepared to ask for adjournment. But before I could accede to the chairman's judgment, a cry of support began to rise cautiously from those in attendance. Soon it became a roar. They were all on their feet, unanimous—except for one—that my character needed no endorsement by the chairman. In a furious instant, the storm passed. The sun shone more brightly than ever. I was not only acquitted, but celebrated.

We had lived for a while in our new house. Suddenly it seemed odd to the congregation that they had never had a housewarming for us. All this changed. Here was a splendid excuse for them to say,

"We love you!" Perhaps they were really saying, "We're sorry." It seemed they knew they had been silent too long. They gathered around us, not to ask us if they could have a housewarming, but to tell us when they would do it.

The inglorious season had ended.

The utter pain that had nearly separated us from the church came to a singing finale. Could it be? Could Maundy Thursday return again to the glory of Palm Sunday? And yet it had! The chairman of the board had been soundly defeated. In some ways, he seemed rather piteous to me that night. He was handsome and once popular. Now he seemed alone, without support. But we were alive and we had discovered one great vitality. We could handle pain and the stress of our worst days could be managed. And more than that, we were set free in a kind of love we would never again have to doubt. We could live without anything but each other.

They never knew I had carried a written resignation into the pulpit and brought it home again. The resignation, all prepared and signed, was still in my coat. The dark night of the soul had come and gone, and we had survived. I kissed you in the darkness, just inside the door of the parsonage. I left the funny, folded paper in my pocket, still unread. I crumpled it into a little ball, hoping that I would remember to throw it away before I took the suit to the cleaners.

Life began anew, resurrected from despair. It seemed that we were now free to live and, one day, to die—still together. The first half of our lives had been declared. We had managed the dash across the burning bridge to the second part of life, and we were not afraid of church members anymore. We were not afraid of board chairmen anymore. We belonged to Christ and to each other, and whatever the rest of our lives should hold, we knew we would traverse it clinging to the hope that Robert Browning cheered:

> *Grow old along with me!*
> *The best is yet to be,*
> *The last of life, for which the first was made.*
>   *("Rabbi Ben Ezra")*

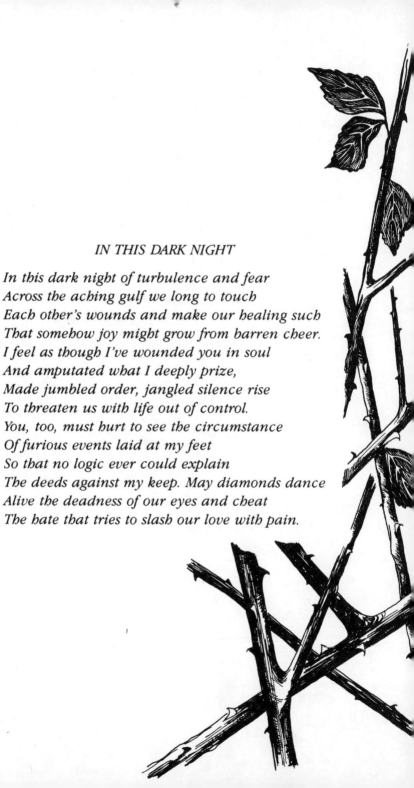

IN THIS DARK NIGHT

In this dark night of turbulence and fear
Across the aching gulf we long to touch
Each other's wounds and make our healing such
That somehow joy might grow from barren cheer.
I feel as though I've wounded you in soul
And amputated what I deeply prize,
Made jumbled order, jangled silence rise
To threaten us with life out of control.
You, too, must hurt to see the circumstance
Of furious events laid at my feet
So that no logic ever could explain
The deeds against my keep. May diamonds dance
Alive the deadness of our eyes and cheat
The hate that tries to slash our love with pain.

14

$\mathscr{T}$INTAGEL

Once the children were gone, we both stopped to question life as we were living it. "Late and soon, getting and spending we lay waste out powers," said Wordsworth. We suddenly were besought by feelings of failure. Had we given our lives for these many years in the best possible way? We needed healing and a time away from the church for reflecting on our use of those years already spent and those to come as well. The love of Christ seemed remote, and suddenly our missing youth seemed a lost expenditure.

My soul and outlook were healed at the same time. When life was whole again, we decided to take a trip to England. There are few sights lovelier than the English countryside. We drove from London, aimlessly north and west and then south again. At last we stood at the remote, southwest edge of England. My interest in Malory and other strains of lore about King Arthur had compelled us here. Tintagel had called to me as surely as the wild coasts of Cornwall rose against the gray sea. I had been intrigued by the legendary hero of England's romantic past. What doubt and stir King Arthur once had made! Some say he never was. There was no Camelot, they say, unless the splendid court met in a primitive fortress made all of wood, now burned or lost.

In my youth, I much idealized King Arthur. My fascination as a man dulled to mere interest until I actually stood in Cornwall. There on the windswept plateau, I was forced to admit there is a kind of magic in the very geography of Tintagel.

I never will forget the gray, clear morning that we stood on the wide and rolling hills, as austere as the turbulent water they defied. Here where the land was at an end, we were drawn to the perimeter of an ancient world—where Uther Pendragon had once slept with the lady Igraire and sired either a king or a captivating myth.

But the eighteenth year of our marriage had brought a need to break the fatiguing realities that had pulled us from each other. Is it possible that the unanswered riddles of all those who wrote on the myth of Arthur drew us to England? I think not. It was the romance of all our reading that drew us to this place.

The green fields of Cornwall had carried us to the tumbledown ruins of England's most ancient castle. And here was the ecstasy Geoffrey of Monmouth used to substantiate the rationale of eight hundred years of British tourists and two centuries of American.

We had suffered far too much reality—the service of Christ had become a stark ministry too void of fantasy and life. Here was place to feed imagination as it delivered us from the daily round. The dryads never danced; there were no centaurs or dragons or ladies-in-waiting. But here the humdrum grew holy. I had once written that dull circumstances need bright unicorns or there will be only horses:

Unicorns are garish horses
void of browns and grays.
We let them live because we fear
the humdrum of our days.
(The Song)

We scaled the black cliffs of Cornwall and scanned the chosen trail of legends. Like the Loch Ness creature, they eluded us. Arthur was gone, and none who told his story had spoken of ordinary things, but only of such things as fed our begging imagination. Magic swords and round tables make life bearable. What needs of heart or mystery had brought us to this place of wild enchantment? Was there not a nearer way to ease our soul-fatigue? Why England? Why didn't God extend His perfect peace to us without our ever leaving town? Yet in the truest sense, He did. It was God who, working in our lives, had solved our problems. Still, His answers are rarely immediate. We had prayed and sought God who left us longing for His absolute reality. We were often angry at Him because of His silence. Ill at ease in our own need, we cried like Job in our pursuit of Him: "O that I knew where I might find Him."

At Tintagel, we met Him in a new way. We saw how He could use the gift of imagination to make us believe in both ourselves and Him. Yes, imagination and romance are somehow necessary in life. Life needs a little help, sometimes.

It is the cry of every man born again from desolation, "Give me back my dreams so I may live!" No wonder the prophet declared, "Where there is no vision, the people perish" (Proverbs 29:18). Having seen reality up close, it was healing to stop and celebrate a legend. T. H. White's epigraph came to me as I stood in the salt-washed air, above the sea:

Hic Iacet Arthurus
Rex quondem Rexque Futurus
(The Once and Future King)

How easy it was to believe Christ in England. How easy it was to amend *Rex Futurus* to *Rex Adessus,* "The once and *present* king."

To be sure, I knew who the real King was. The power of Christ still lived in us and surged till the deadness was gone. Our love was as alive as England itself. And He, the King, once and present, had done it all.

I kissed you there in the salty sea air. Our misery and our disconsolation was healed once again. Christ had indeed been with us, but not too soon. For our sakes, he had hidden His Kingship so that beyond our barren days, we could behold His power to make dead men live again. We submitted and were free!

TINTAGEL

Where sleeps your King tonight, you silent stones?
Will you not cry and speak, dumb clotted earth,
Alive with words? Your aching silence groans
And weeps to know the truth of Arthur's birth.
Or would we know? Did Merlyn cause your fall?
Did Mordred stride this moonlit, roofless room?
Did Guinevere once pace this crumbling hall
That soon became the famous table's tomb?
Let dead Excalibur spark legend fire.
Do we not need a fable here and there?
Some wider themes of lost nobility?
Ideals like crosses penetrate the air.
It seems unwise to doubt dead Lancelot,
For life foams mad, outside of Camelot.

15

THE TWENTIETH WINTER

Winter is our special time, but this cold current season summons up again a winter now twenty years past. The distant winter witnessed our engagement. We had rented a car in Toronto and driven to the falls. The night held, as Shakespeare said, an eager and a biting air. The impetuous, green Niagara River fell from Erie to Ontario. We stood at the rail to watch its hurried fall.

How can you force two days twenty years apart to stand together? Here we were, traveling to Niagara in our early forties to celebrate an event born on a cold Oklahoma day. On the Queen Elizabeth Way, we drove a 1979 Pontiac, but on that day when we could not dream of 1979, we had driven 1951 Chevrolet. I gave you a ring and made you a promise and you accepted both in the winter of '59.

Now it was twenty years since you had taken the diamond. I had concealed a second diamond in the pocket of my mackinaw. Another ring—a way of pulling the years together with promises, I believed. I had begged the later and smaller diamond to bear witness to the first. It was a ring for your other hand, a small stone of witness. As we were older, so were the promises of 1959. Of course, we had known winters of discontent, but they had yielded joyously in time to better seasons.

Life had become a celebration. I tried to lay your younger face above your present visage. The mask was somehow undersize—we were bigger for our years. Nothing of your inner light had diminished, your eyes were much brighter, your smile more free.

The water roared. It was winter, yet the gulls were there. They cried and turned and rose. Where were their forebears that soared above the cascades in 1959? I knew that afternoon that every promise was important. I could see the fickle waters in their northward hurry. They ran and swirled toward Quebec as though Canada would give them a freedom they had not found in the United States. How well they matched the impetuous, restless search of early marriage. Their unsteady turbulence was so unsure of the last state of their merger with a calmer sea.

In 1959, I had slipped the ring on your finger and said, "For better or for worse . . . I will always love you, cherish, and honor you . . . ." I had meant the vow, but I had not lived up to it well. Who makes a promise to cherish and always cherishes? Who pledges love and always loves? Yes, a thousand times in those past years I had not been as loving as I had promised, a thousand, thousand times I had not cherished or esteemed you. But our marriage held because all promises hold their own integrity. Though we who pledge are weak, the promises secure our wavering intentions.

Twenty years before, I had made the same kind of promises to God. I told Him He could have my life and I would forever serve Him. Yet I had vacillated between my pledge to Him and my own self-will. I ever gave and snatched back my commitment to Christ. Yet He must have known that the intent of my life was to serve Him, even when I acted in my own interest. And like Him, you received my pledge and discovered that, while I was not always loving, honoring, and cherishing you, our conflicts were dissolved in those two-decade promises that somehow managed to live on in spite of our misdirected wills.

The falls were deserted, and we were gloriously alone. We were triumphant. We had outwitted the crowds! What madness made them come in the sultry summer? We had been to Niagara only once in summer and despised ourselves for our judgment. Winter was for us a perfect time for setting the decades straight. We watched the water, and then I turned and slipped the glove from your hand. The glove was cold, but your hand felt warm. I placed a second ring and looked at it in the cold mist until the frost forced you to replace your glove. We walked along the rail, then turned back to our hotel. We could not bring the years together, really. The decades still stood far apart. We were older, but the years were worth the aging. We knew now what we could not have known twenty years before: love is not worthy of the name unless it can endure the test of twenty winters. A great deal of pain had passed beneath our faces. What would life be like when future decades passed? The winters would mark each anniversary and set us free to remember that the weather is never unfriendly. The snow but whitens the hair and thins the skin. And every value grows more dear when improved with age. The hearth is warmer in the shorter winters of our later, better years.

Winter knows no requiems—it ever celebrates the spring. It tends to freeze the memory as it awakens the world to hope. I know the laws of renunciation. Yet winter encourages its loves to sweet hedonism. The cold stands at the corners of the room and makes us love the fire that blazes at the center. Come, December! We want to snuggle, once again, beneath an afghan and hypnotize our souls with dancing flames. Here love feeds best. Bread is so tasteless in summer. Stars never really shine until the snow has cleaned the air; then distant galaxies bleed through the cold skies, and silence absorbs all sounds and starlight.

A million hurts were ours from winter unto winter.

Did your mother die in those fast-fleeing seasons? Did our unborn children come and grow to be the wiry shadows of ourselves? Did a war in Southeast Asia wax and wane? Six presidents came and went throughout the years we measure. Yet here are diamonds that witness twenty years and will not let our union be divided.

TWO DIAMONDS TWO DECADES APART

The frost hung there—do you remember how
The January air stung your young face?
With all the warmth the wind chill would allow,
I kissed you by the cedars. The embrace
Was all I needed to confirm the vow.
I slipped the cold small ring inside your glove.
The tiny frozen stone said, "Wait, for now."
My promise glistened on the seal of love.
The years fled by and stole our youth. We heard
Our children cry—beheld our parents die.
Where have the flowers gone? Was it absurd
To let the frozen decades pass us by?
For twenty winters I have loved you so.
I long to find you diamonds in the snow.

16

THE FAR GATES

The winters of our discontent were comfortably separated by happier summers. None of the problems that beset us were big—only routine. Still, a thousand little bandits may carry away as much as a grand larcenist. The demon of fatigue bedding with the strain of raising adolescents made for a troubled sleep.

When the days grew long for both of us, there yet came the nights when little decisions had to be made, small judgments passed. Were they teenagers for only seven years? Those were seven fat years for them and seven leans ones for us. Like the cows of Joseph's dream, the fat years oft devoured the lean.

It wasn't just telling them that some conduct was approved or some attitude unacceptable that made the days so wearing. It was the heavy feeling of competition that often ended in struggles as though we were somehow enemies. We wouldn't have had it that way. The exercising of our finest wisdom they judged incompetent. They rarely spoke their malcontent, but the looks, the heavy footfalls, the silences at the table were blatant. There were always the small contests met by flashes of resentment. And there were longer week-to-week, year-to-year issues met by solid viewpoints from which neither we nor they yielded.

It was all a regular part of raising children. Still, for me, the years were a time of unending strain. And for us, I could tell that the struggles of adolescence drove wedges of pain between us. Motherhood is a category that sides deeply and consistently with adolescence. Fatherhood gets tired quicker. Motherhood understands when fatherhood rages. Motherhood is willing to give situations another chance, forgiving seventy times seven. Fatherhood declares itself, legislates, and makes rules that seal the children from the father.

To be sure, children must be their own persons, and I always desired mine to be. But their seize-and-destroy path to the twenties, I found, passed haltingly the broad fields of anger and moved out into the deserts of silence. When the upper slopes of real confrontation came, I began to hope for abdication.

You could always handle so much more than I. You believed that someday it would again be like it used to be. You trusted that one day, when they had laid aside their need to contest every decision, to cut their way to independence, life would be sweet again. You trusted the book of Proverbs and Mark Twain's dictum that once they were a little older, they would see how very intelligent we had become—all at once.

I can see that in most ways their challenges were normal. They never trespassed civil law nor declared themselves communists or ran off with lovers to live soap-opera lives. They never forced us to reckon with damaged reputations. They studied hard, made good grades, and enjoyed college.

But the deepest contests were always rooted in issues of their destinies. What could they become if they could dream better? What were they contemplating that might hurt their studies or their futures? Their hostility rose quickly and seemed without a foundation. They confronted us often just because we were there and in some ways seemed to grasp greedily the reins of family life. They had a way of making the least matters seem like power struggles, yet we were gentle in our use of power.

It was not our confrontations with them that began at last to weary me. It was the fact that I felt fatigue edging into our own relationship. The bright conversations of early marriage seemed to degenerate into business as usual. Dutifully we went to band concerts or choral concerts at school. The football games and dances that you often chaperoned were for me not so much wearisome as an intrusion into a busy church schedule that left us so little time for ourselves.

The lawn was big and I gave myself to the dreary mowing of it. The house, the laundry, the work you did constantly at school in the mornings and in the evenings. The church, the counseling appointments, the council meetings, the business meetings, the conventions, the days that kept us so busy that they ended with our collapsing into bed at night.

I remembered so often those days the myth of Sisyphus. I can see the titan: damned as he was to an eternity of misery, his crime so offensive to the gods that he was sentenced to a meaninglessness from which there was no exit. He must roll a huge boulder up the slopes of a steep mountain, only to watch it tumble and roll to the bottom again. Then he must descend the mountain and push it up again and so on, forever.

Meaninglessness always has no exit—no reasonable way out. I could picture this hulk of a demigod, straining his whole body, lifting and pushing and daring to believe there was meaning in the moment. His cheek against the stone, his foot wedging it in, all to bear it to the top one more weary time. How many times in eternity does he reach the meaningless summit? In the unholy humdrum, there is no difference between the top and the bottom. There are no goals, no prizes in such a predictable world.

But those years taught me much about the nature of life. Its great curse is never the effort, but the unanswered effort. No wonder Sartre had defined his hero as the man who could look at the meaninglessness of life and decide to keep on living.

To leave a pit, one must ever remember the steep sides and convince himself that the tiny fleck of light high above must not be lost. For when the climb is over, that barely visible pinpoint of light will open into a world of sky and earth where the grass is tender and the world is young and hope is as certain as the breeze.

Sensitivity may be my own rock on the slopes of the hill. I feel things so deeply. My depression settles ever deeper than yours. My elation rises higher—or so it seems on the surface. I articulate quickly what you ponder and often leave unsaid. Because of my own visible moods, my utter rejection of the routine was outwardly more venomous. I begin to see why so many men in the twentieth year of marriage could no longer cope with the fatigue and the strain of a home where they often felt they only made mortgage payments, but held no place.

Now that I really consider it, I know you bore your own separate loneliness. You reached so regularly to stabilize the children as they teetered on the various precipices of their teenage years. Yet at the same time, you tried to reach for me to celebrate the ordinary things that ought to have brought me more joy than they did.

It began to occur to me: Sisyphus was more than a myth. Not unlike myself, he took himself too seriously. Who knows but if he enjoyed his life of exhibitionism and even gloried in his observable pain? Was not some of the tedium of his life his own fault? Could he not see it? At noon one day there must have come a butterfly to rest upon his stone. And for one moment, the humdrum is enlivened by bright transcending wings.

Do you recall my reflections on Sisyphus during one of the drudging seasons?

We are tied to micro-tasks: bitter vinegar and gall,

Hoping for the larger moments, doomed to live among the small.

We would be presidents or kings, building towers for artful skies,
Smiling while the pawns hack pawns, for the bishops' enterprise.

But the laundry! God, the laundry! Done a thousand times, but here once more.
The factory eating up our stamina with rivets, driven hard with heat and gore.
In the same plates, mind you, that we've riveted before.
Rivets, hundreds of them, years and years of rivets. . . .

Sisyphus, you blind and mundane dolt!

You missed the butterfly. So had I. The tedium was not our curse, nor was the children's adolescence. The curse, like the blessing, lay within ourselves, because we willingly enter the dull dungeons of our hearts.

The tedium that we so despised was not our curse but our salvation. The lawn and the laundry redeemed. At last, I could see the product in the tedium. The regularity of things that must be done often mortars our best ideas.

We could be healed. Jesus said:

Consider the lilies of the fields, how they grow; they toil not, neither do they spin: And yet I say unto you, That even Solomon in all his glory was not arrayed like one of these. (Matthew 6:28–29)

I saw you again in a new way the summer that our children finished high school. We were in the mountains. Do you remember the field of lilies? I was painting, and I scooped a handful of them and tore them from the ground. Their dangling roots held the moist mountain earth. But their heads were white as though they had never beheld any stain. I looked at the exquisite flowers, and in them, I understood the glory of our freedom. I painted them. But who can truly capture on canvas that which God alone creates? Their delicate beauty eluded brush and oil. Nonetheless, I worked the color, and as I did, I remembered Jesus' words. I retraced the steps a thousand times to lay the oil upon the canvas. Somehow each time my brush dipped into the messy palette, it rose again and left me freer. Here lay the truth of the summer of 1980: There are no anxious lilies. They bear no strain—debate no longing views of life. There are only free, white flowers that work together to blanket a mountainside. "Yet Solomon in all his glory was not arrayed like one of these."

I knew the stress within our marriage could be put to rest. I began to understand that inner peace came as a result of pulling down the high walls of my demands in our marriage. I saw that you were torn by trying to handle two jobs at once. The no-man's-land between your older lover and your younger lovers kept you from feeling adequate for either of them.

In the pain of their growing, our children were becoming what we were: adults. And I smiled and I knew that this was exactly how they saw us. They were becoming adults, and we were only becoming old. What a foolish misjudgment was theirs!

Now I could tell them. There are no adults. Adults are children who reach out for love and cry out to be touched. Adults are not postadolescent—not beings cured of teenager-hood. Adults are caught in the lifelong struggle of wondering what to do with their superior maturity. They are plagued by feelings that they are children forced to dress up and play for real at a game they barely understand. They ache in the realization that the bright prophecies of their youth are not being fulfilled.

This victory was not one of mind alone! At the end of that fateful summer, we were both free in a new way. The good things had early taught us that love would never be surrendered. We would not stand together against our children—we would stand together *for* them. But we would stand together!

Our new resolve was declared neither to ourselves nor to our children. But everyone knew the new precepts. The days sped by. The laundry came and went by loads. Lawnmowers did their work. Yet, there was a freshness in the toughness of our well-trodden paths; we were free as the lilies. We had given life our best effort and the best product was our two children, now leaving childhood only to find that they can never leave. And we were, like Hansel and Gretel, confident in our trust that even in the midst of a dark forest, the witches could all be beaten.

A SOLDIER AND A MAID

They left us both at once, became as one
The age for leaving . . . and yet, didn't they
Seem young? We woke them from their naps to run
And they leapt decades on one summer day.
They hurried off with luggage, nothing more!
Were his shoes tied? Did he forget his lunch?
And did her ribbons match her pinafore?
They walked alone. Where was their childish bunch?
The silence roars and gels the unstirred gloom.
And dare we draw the noisy lock and chain
To seal ourselves in all these empty rooms?
Can our door-watching bring the joy again?
This lonely night we have our debts all paid
And given life a soldier and a maid.

17

THE SILVER PLEDGE

After all these years, I wonder now at my reluctance to become engaged to you. The love I feared to define had defined itself in the years that were required to write the definition. We celebrate our growth by smiling at our outgrown concepts.

We have lived together long enough to know that we were made to live together. Gone is any false attempt to recreate each other in some image that we might find more acceptable. Having left our needs to change each other, life is a celebration of ourselves as we are.

We are free, complete in each other, and it is not dull company. We are filled with a fullness that guards against its own spillage. When we are together, we are content because our communication needs no larger audience than ourselves. We have learned that loneliness inhabits crowds. When the streets hold only us, the sidewalks are content.

Remember the cataracts of Niagara? The falls flowed on, like time itself. The water held one grandiose desire: to roll through the St. Lawrence Seaway and be free of the restrictive channel that created the river. Every river is but an ocean in process, and oceans are rivers so wide and full they cannot go back. Our marriage, like a river, ever seeks a wider place.

The dark cascades that roared across our early years have moved on. There is a crispness already in the air that reminds us that we can not have summer forever. One day, one of us will be forced to stand alone and test the shattering emptiness that is the final fruit of those who knew closeness.

Our little woes may give way to bigger ones— maybe disease, perhaps infirmity. Are we up to the future? The now must not be frightened by those fears that make us die before we've lived each day to the fullest. We must be fully alive in the present and stay alive until we have to say goodbye. Someone once remarked that the future is much like the present—only longer. Neither the future nor the present is a terror to those who walk as one.

Our commitments were never showy. I have despised to give you kisses or gifts in public. We kept the best events of life between ourselves. The years moved on by troops, and this December, not in impatience, our days are still full. We are at our best still when we are alone, not observed, not exhibitionist in our loving. We rarely spend ourselves in giving gifts. Time is our gift—yes, and being. There is no need for presents when life itself is a present.

Even now as I write, I know the children will soon be home from the university. Our days will be heaped with extra levels of fullness. Then the "two-ness" that we so enjoy will become, instantly and comfortably, a "fourness."

And shortly after Christmas, the holiday will end upon a midnight. On that eve, the clock will remind us that another year has dawned—our twenty-fifth. It will bid us to stay alive by honoring some old and certain covenants. The midnight clock will remind us that time is a gift to keep only while we live, and live we shall. As the ghost of Christmas Present reminded Ebenezer: "There is never enough time and suddenly you're not there anymore." But the shortness of life will not hurry us along to moroseness. We will seek joy without cramming all the goodies of this life quickly into our pockets, as though there were no more. To understand the swiftness of life is to live in youth. And sometimes I think we are younger in our forties than we ever were in early marriage.

And in the cycle of change, each year—with its beauty and intrigue—passes on, stealing from us, bit by bit, as we celebrate its passage. Since first we met, a hundred seasons have come and gone. None of them could make us fear. Each one, in passing, summoned up our great desire to meet the next.

Our greatest joys are simple: the rock hearth in February, the small fountain on our patio, the flowering crab apple tree, the walks in summer, the fall colors of the river forests we love. These both celebrate the past and reach with eagerness ahead. Living fully in the now is the only way to keep the years from becoming the skeletons of old, dull schedules.

Let me watch you making tea on cold mornings.

Tease the puppy in the garden. Cover the geraniums against first frost. I want to watch these simple acts mortar moments into life. Thus is tomorrow born again, ninety times in every season.

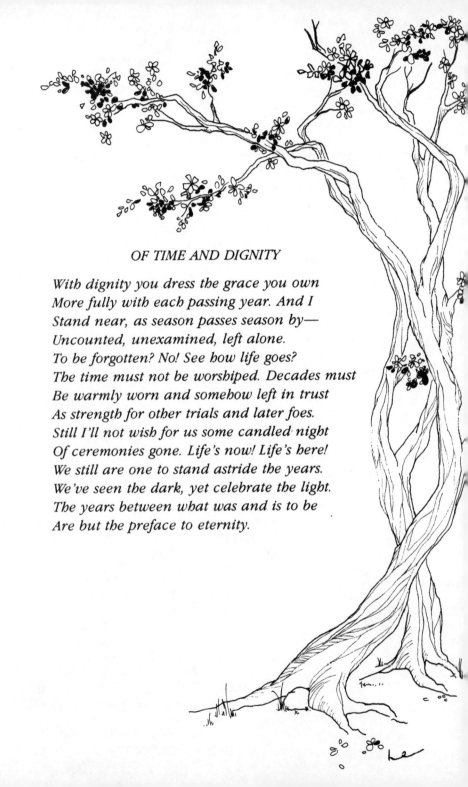

OF TIME AND DIGNITY

With dignity you dress the grace you own
More fully with each passing year. And I
Stand near, as season passes season by—
Uncounted, unexamined, left alone.
To be forgotten? No! See how life goes?
The time must not be worshiped. Decades must
Be warmly worn and somehow left in trust
As strength for other trials and later foes.
Still I'll not wish for us some candled night
Of ceremonies gone. Life's now! Life's here!
We still are one to stand astride the years.
We've seen the dark, yet celebrate the light.
The years between what was and is to be
Are but the preface to eternity.